DAMN, YOU STILL SINGLE?

A Self-Help Guide to Navigating Singlehood from "Never Again to My Man, My Man, My Man.

NIKKI FRIAS

Cover Photo: Rahman Harper
Book Design by Our Galaxy Publishing

ISBN 979-8-218-41781-9 (paperback)

www.girltellme.com

This book is dedicated to the girl spending hours on her hair and makeup for a first date at Buffalo Wild Wings on Football Sunday, the guy anxiously waiting for a text about the 9 pm reservations, or anyone else who deleted a dating app for the 3rd time this month.

Let the current dumpster fire state of the world be an indicator that being single is the least of your (and my) problems.

"Damn, You Still Single?"

A Self-Help Guide to Navigating Singlehood from
"Never Again" to My Man, My Man, My Man.

A Word to the Reader

Chapter One: POST-DIVORCE..3
The consolation prize of divorce is clarity.

Chapter Two: SINGLE AF..21
Driving the streets, backroads and avenues of dating.

Chapter Three: MINGLE..45
The lessons from dating debauchery, in no particular order.

Chapter Four: GIVING UP..105
The realities learned from throwing all the fish back in the sea.

Chapter Five: FALLING IN LOVE.......................................129
Learning from a small window of time.

Chapter Six: TAKEN...139
"My man, my man, my man."

A Word to the Reader

Well, well, well, we meet again!

First off: Hey, Bitch. *How we doing?*

Let me start off by thanking you for paying my bills and supporting my words yet again! If you're new here, please take a seat. We have much to cover in the amount of time it takes you to finish this book. Let me emphasize: bitches never finish books (I'm bitches). I would've read this page and immediately put the book down for TikTok, Instagram, or to eat another salty snack instead of dinner.

As I live by my own principles of being a "Do Something" bitch, I bring to you another book following *Does This Divorce Make Me Look Fat?* I'll assume you know the story, but if you don't…stop being cheap and buy the book already. As the self-proclaimed "Judy Blume for Bitches" it's my pleasure to write yet another in hopes it will empower you, your mom, or the table you put it down on and never came back to.

When writing *Does this Divorce Make Me Look Fat?* I wrote 10 pages and didn't touch it again for three years. Similarly, now, *Damn, You Still Single?* has been a rollercoaster of emotions. For context, my original draft read like I was Uma Thurman in *Kill Bill*, but instead of actual characters, every negative thought about my future in love was kicking my ass. Some chapters sounded bitter, and others lacked hope. While therapeutic, it felt inauthentic to who I was and what I wanted this book to feel like by the end.

Aside from the fluency in Fuck Boy, expertise in "blocked," and specialty in spotting red flags, the clarity that you'll find in every chapter came from the process of unlearning what I was told and relearning what I wanted. The structure of this book follows the eight-year journey from post-divorce to now a healthy relationship after overcoming internal conflicts, and the acceptance that what I want looks different in my own evolution.

If you're reading this thinking, "This funny lady's going to give me all the tricks of the trade to find a good ass man with chuckles along the way!" Return it. This book is not about the *dos* and *don'ts* of dating; it's about the lessons I've learned with mending a broken heart while simultaneously trying to find myself before finding love again. Not to mention the indifferent feelings of being vulnerable, the struggles of bouncing back after another failed talking stage, and the exhaustion that comes with feeling too old to make mistakes in dating but also too young to give up entirely.

Damn, You Still Single? is a comedic reflective book dedicated to the girls that sing "No Scrubs" at Karaoke night like their life depends on it, eye-roll at yet another "we're engaged" photo, or gag at the thought of answering, "What are you looking for?" for the umpteenth time.

Lastly, anticipate some explanations for words throughout the book noted as a "Hector Hint." This comes as a response to my 70-year-old father, who previously mentioned he didn't get the references to some of the slang used in my first book. Anything for you, Dad.

Chapter One:

POST-DIVORCE.

The consolation prize of divorce is clarity.

Post-Divorce: One Year Out

I've survived...

It's been a year since I divorced and I've since moved to New York City with no job, no friends, and no family to help with the process of "figuring it out." The shock of my ex-husband having a baby on the side is almost nonexistent. I sometimes forget I used to be married. It's such an odd feeling to look back on the last 10 years with a person like a movie I was never supposed to star in.

The months following my move have been the saddest I've experienced since the day I found out. I'd never hurt or unalive myself, but now I understand the difficulty of my own sadness. I expected it to come from the snippets of my old life on Facebook or the retelling of stories, but never the silence. Therapy has helped, but since I've moved, my mental health has taken a hit from the loneliness that follows living in a new space with nothing. Even living in the loudest city amongst the honking and people yelling, the only thing I've been able to hear is my internal battles. For now, these four walls of my Brooklyn apartment, and my dog have bear witness to the mourning, learning, reminding, and accepting of who I am after the decree was finalized.

The hardest part has been accepting my newly found freedom. It's terrifying to think about the responsibility of making my own decisions without having another person. I'm dreading the awkwardness of sex with someone new, being flirty on a first date, or navigating a new world alone. Even unhappy, overweight, and miserable, the comfort of a partner means I could bury my traumas by deciding what's for dinner or making weekend plans. Instead, I'm confronting my fear of being unloved, what role love plays in my life, and where this lingering sadness comes from.

I keep telling myself this time will pass, but this year has felt like a lifetime. I know one day I'll feel more like myself, it's just this chapter of my life has been the hardest to understand. They say, "God gives his hardest battles to the toughest soldiers," but this feels more like a draft and I'm already ready to retire.

now what?

Mourning: The life I thought I had.

And here lies the woman who thought she had it all.

Even before I was married, my idea of what life would look like was based on the narrative that princesses were picked by princes, and the gift of belonging to someone meant a life with meaning where my ovaries united in the world of fertility. I'd lose my shoes and live barefoot in the kitchen quickly after. Nothing says societal success like pushing out a watermelon and claiming it on your taxes, amirite? My white picket fence would come in the form of a NYC loft apartment. We'd have one baby (maybe), and countless "young and dumb" stories that no one asked to hear. It started and ended with being chosen.

I rarely made decisions for myself in love from an early age to my present-day failed marriage. In high school, I liked who liked me. Hence the embarrassment when I now get a direct message or friend request (Yes, I'm on Facebook. I am a millennial.) from yet another fashion brand "entrepreneur" (aka sells t-shirts) from my hometown. Even at a young age, once I was chosen, I'd change my looks, dress differently, talk less, and try to do things to remain picked. A "pick me*" person before it was a thing, my infatuation of being in a relationship led to the bad habits I practiced well into my late 20s.

Once married, our life had all the things promised from being chosen: football Sundays at our house, game nights, an adopted dog, travel, and all the material things we could attain with a dual income. This was my reward: the wedding, friends and family, the house. We were THAT couple amongst our friend group. The "I want that kind of love" or "I hope to have what you have" type of couple. Little did they know I was suffering.

The responsibilities and efforts needed to sustain our image were normally met with misunderstanding and unhappiness behind closed doors. I'd lay on the floor of our home and let the teardrops dry down my cheek, blaming my period for my unexpected behavior. I lessened myself to be a "Mrs." and now didn't know who I was or what I wanted following the first year of marriage. I did all the "things" to be kept, and now I silently had to accept that the sacrifice of being chosen meant I had to settle for the life I thought I wanted (but didn't), with a man I didn't want.

The eight-year investment I had with this person meant the hard decision of leaving or changing my life was doubtful. Instead, I accepted the repercussions of not sticking up for myself in the form of bland sex and feeling isolated in my marriage til death did us part. I was miserable in this chosen life, but it seemed better than the latter; single and alone.

I spent years defending my relationship to family, so the success of my marriage was to prove them wrong. I faked my happiness amongst friends in group settings and pushed myself into the mindset that the hard times would be rewarded with couple's trips to Jamaica. Things would eventually change. It was easier to live in denial than the reality of my choices. So much that when I initially found out about the infidelity, I blamed her and justified his behavior to my lack of sex drive and depressive weight gain. The fear of the unknown outweighed my independence, so I stayed and tried to make it work until he told me she was pregnant. Then, I had no choice. I made the big-girl decision to leave the marriage for good. Like I said, get the first book. It's juicy.

I had a get-out-of-jail-free card, but never anticipated what I'd do when it was given.

Unprepared to process my failed marriage, a wave of shame and guilt came over me. Shame from the times I stuck up for his mediocre behavior and thought I was untouchable and the guilt of accepting a life I chose out of fear. Most of my decisions were made out of what someone else saw for my life, and I felt like I could no longer trust myself to make decisions that were in my best interest. My identity was so wrapped up in the idea that keeping a man meant I mattered, I didn't know what I would do without one.

As a response to any tragedy, I mourned. This was after all the numbers were blocked, family-in-laws unfriended on social media, and any other form of contact was non-existent. I created all the boundaries, and it was time to be still. The uncharted territory of saying goodbye to my marriage, my old life, some friends, and the normalcy of that comfort was difficult to accept. I tried to explain it to friends and family, but no one can really understand the instant change when it's not something they've experienced.

Mourning looked like crying in bed to daydreaming about the good times. Some days, I'd be so angry at myself and others over how he ruined our lives. I had to come to terms with my life looking different than expected and with the understanding that, while scary, I had to learn it by myself. I wasn't ready to be the big girl I bragged about, but I knew if I stayed, I would lose the last bit of dignity I had.

The beautiful thing about mourning was unlearning the idea that keeping a man gave me purpose. I had a choice in the matter, and the power to accept what I wanted in all aspects of my life.

Admittedly, I would judge women who were cheated on or had broken relationships, and now we're all single drunkenly complimenting each other's hair in the bathroom on a Saturday night. Instead of focusing on wasted time, I forgave myself for the almost 10 years on autopilot and flipped the script on remaining picked. A gut punch to myself, my dignity, and the picture-perfect life I thought I had, I failed at remaining picked by picking myself.

Mourn the idea of what you assumed for your life. There might be something better on the other side of choosing yourself.

Sure, I can't keep a man, but I will never lose myself again.

*Hector Hint: "Pick me" is a girl who desires to be chosen. It's used as a negative connotation since most are outwardly desperate and aggressively seeking attention, but for me my insecurities led my decisions.

Learning: Good things happen to shit people.

This one hurts a little.

I always prided myself on being morally good. I'd recycle, tip graciously, return shopping carts, and when I'm in a really giving mood, I'd let student drivers merge over. A believer in karma and the benefits of doing the right thing, I struggled to understand how my ex-husband was rewarded with what he always wanted: a baby, job, family, and home. He's supposed to be miserable for a couple years before bouncing back with that one girl from high school who sells Scentsy or nail stickers*.

I always assumed doing the right thing would please the universe and I'd have a leg up when it came to life, but my ex-husband was a reminder that good things still happen to shit people. I remember when I was going through my divorce, people would say, "He'll get what's coming to him," or "Karma's a bitch," but maybe not. Maybe he'd never see the errors of his ways or reap what was sowed. Instead, he's thriving and the happiest he's ever been.

I hoped he'd find his happiness, but debunking my logic of good behavior granting me anything was hard to wrap my head around. I remember my bullies from high school, even while being the spawns of Satan, they still had the best hair, cutest kids, and biggest friend groups with the pictures on social media to prove it. Yes, we can agree social media is a facade, but there is some form of happiness in their lives.

I'd compare and shake my fist to the sky at the idea of not getting what was owed to me. I'd wonder why I had the emotional burden of fixing myself while yet another "friend" was celebrating their engagement, taking another trip, or starting a new lucrative job.

I prided myself on being highly favored for all the good I put into the world, like volunteering during the holidays or unplugging my vampire electronics. My assumption of being rewarded was winning the lottery, a beautiful new rich man, or carbs making me lose weight, but instead, it was a kept job, good health, and a working car. I expected more than everyone else and hated on whoever had more than me in love, money, or career.

Unfortunately, the more I compared and thought of people as undeserving of love, life, and success based off my own judgements, the more I discredited the other good in my life—from health, mindset, mental clarity, loving family and friends, bills paid to a full tank of gas. Learning that good behavior was just good behavior helped me understand my "why." It wasn't to be granted amenities; it was simply who I was.

Great things happen to shit people, but most importantly, great things are happening to you. Don't take for granted the other things you've been given instead of what you expected for the specific time in your life. Comparing yourself to whoever you deem as unworthy based on what you do or don't have is a disservice to yourself and the person you're judging. Instead, remember you're most deserving, and whatever you want you will have regardless of how disappointing people can be. The good and bad things happen to everyone. It's how we define the good we already have that matters.

Keep donating that dollar toward childhood diabetes at the movie theater, his goofy ass still thriving.

*Hector Hint: Scentsy is a multi-level marketing product that has candle parties, and nail stickers are stickers you put on your fingernails instead of nail polish.

Reminding: Healing is cyclical.

"What goes up, must come down."

I dreaded dates: our wedding date, his birthday, Christmas, and the anniversary of our becoming official. These dates were celebrated for ten years with parties, extravagant gifts, and trips.

The first year, I forgot our anniversary. The second year, I didn't realize his birthday til 10pm. The third year, I spent Christmas with new traditions. The fourth year, I remembered my wedding anniversary, but on the wrong day. The fifth year, I remembered his birthday, but also spent the day on the beach at Coney Island with a new love interest. The sixth year, I spent Christmas with close friends. The seventh year, I completely forgot about my anniversary, and the eighth year, I had to be reminded I was once married.

I also hated BBQ anything, particularly Sweet Baby Ray's. I know I might get canceled for it, but for ten years, my house, clothes, and kitchen smelled like Sweet Baby Ray's Barbeque. My memories were from summer cookouts every day on the grill and the thought of him eating hotdogs smothered in BBQ sauce on a potato roll.

The first year, I couldn't stand it. The second year, I still hated it. The third year, I still hated it. The fourth year, eh…maybe with a chicken nugget. The fifth year, I hated it again. The sixth year, I went to a cookout, and someone was eating it and I didn't have to fight the urge to make a face. The seventh and eighth year, I still hated it.

Lastly, I hated sports. There was always a game playing, whether basketball, baseball, hockey, or football. His teams were Washington, DC, anything: the Wizards, Nationals, Capitals, and Commanders.

The first year, I lived in New York, so it never crossed my mind. The second year, never crossed my mind. The third year, didn't have cable, never thought about it. The fourth, fifth, sixth and seventh years, it never crossed my mind. The eighth year, I watched the Super Bowl.

Healing is cyclical. It changes every year. I still remember my marriage memories from time to time. We spent ten years laughing, crying, having sex, and fighting. So, inevitably, he'll pop into my mind when I hear his favorite song or see someone with moobs* (kidding). You don't just forget about a person that was once such a huge part of your life.

While time heals all wounds, the memories never leave, they're just viewed differently every time. Sometimes it's sadness over him, wonders of his new life, and other times I'm forgetful of ever being married or when his birthday is. Your memories are not going anywhere. Let them be reminders of how badass you are.

Memories are meant to be relived, even just for a laugh.

*Hector Hint: Moobs = man boobs.

Accepting "Even Beyonce got cheated On."

Don't let what happened to you, make you.

When I was married, I'd often have date nights with my best friend and her husband. We'd go to karaoke nights where our husbands embarrassingly sipped mixed drinks at the bar while we belted out a drunken version of "Livin' on a Prayer" by Bon Jovi. After a couple more renditions of the 90s songs we never remembered, we finished up and headed home.

One night, particularly after a night of "Drunk in Lurve," a slurred ode to Beyoncé's "Drunk in Love," we started a healthy conversation about infidelity on the drive home. As fitting to the evening song choice, at one point in the conversation my husband confidently said, "Beyoncé got cheated on. No one's safe," to my best friend as they continued down the rabbit hole of what that meant for everyone else. This was during the time of Lemonade, pre-my-divorce, and post-elevator Solange incident*.

He said, "Beyoncé got cheated on. No one's safe."

I'm talking about the absolute bombshell, whose net worth value is in the hundreds of millions, talented, fertile, beautiful, literally never misses a beat, and the queen of the fucking internet had a medium ugly (talented, but medium ugly) man cheat on her quickly after the birth of their first child. Now, before the debate over the type of person she is and the normal issues that come with commitment, all those points are possible, but we are talking about mother fucking Beyoncé Giselle Knowles PEOPLE! If she was disposable, how the fuck was I going to survive? I started eating vegetables and sometimes shaving my legs that winter.

The foreshadowing that he quickly cheated after warped my thought process. We don't know the extent of their marriage or the dynamics that be, but once it was said, I couldn't comprehend the possibility of a relationship without infidelity. Is cheating an accessory to love? And if Beyoncé couldn't keep a man from stepping out, what the hell did that mean for me? I put a lot of my pride into the success of my romantic relationships, so accepting this ideology was devastating.

I was able to get past the ending of my relationship, but the fear of being cheated on in new relationships evolved into insecurities about meaningless details. His phone being on silent, a delayed response from a text message, him getting home late from a night out with friends; I was in a mental prison trying to protect myself from cheating ever happening again that I did everything I could to control it. I'd ask questions ready to discredit his responses, create fake scenarios to make myself feel worse, and find evidence of wrongdoing in every change of his mood without considering a bad day or his own strife. That was too easy.

I didn't want to accept the "all men cheat" narrative, and there are men out there like me who are seeking partnership, connection, communication, and a healthy relationship with one person. People go through shit. I was just looking for someone to consider talking it out or going to therapy instead of falling into another vagina to fix their problems.

I've been cheated on multiple times throughout my relationships in high school and as an adult. Of course, the other person made the decision, but it was common for me to question the role I played as a result of their actions. I did all the things and, going back to the previous chapter of "Learning: Good Things Happen to Shit People," I thought by attending to what I thought were their needs (shaving my coochie semi-regularly and preparing under seasoned dinners sometimes), it wasn't going to happen to me. Then it did. I thought my appearance, cooking abilities, the amount of money I made, and how I threw it back in the bedroom would deter anyone from stepping out. Yet, that was unrealistic and unfair to me.

One night, after a fight with my then-boyfriend about his whereabouts or lackluster response to a midday text message, he said, "I can't keep taking the blame for what your ex-husband did!" Though taken aback by his honesty, he was right. I just never heard it so directly. I thought I tucked my fragility deep enough in the girl's group chat that he would never notice my vulnerabilities. I was recycling bad habits that made my outlook on finding love and relationships disheartening. I was so hardened and resistant to the opportunity of new love that instead of accepting its potential, I'd push people away and end future relationships prematurely. For me to allow myself the peaceful and faithful love I deserved, I had to stop taking cheating so personally.

One of my best friends says, "If you cheat on me, that's a you problem." Taking this and running, I reframed the idea of cheating not being personal, but more of a personal problem, with no number of hot meals, back rubs, compliments, or money stopping anyone's choice. There is some solace in knowing that I could release the stress that came with my inability to control people's actions. Also, the pleasure of walking away scot-free from a cheating spouse meant the opportunity to break up and move on instead of thinking I created the damage that inevitability ruined a person or relationship.

When I first heard, "Beyoncé got cheated on. No one's safe," I wrestled with accepting what that meant for my future in love. Some of the most famous, high-profile relationships have experienced infidelity. While sad, they are a reiteration that no matter who you are, people are going to do what they want. I had to unlearn my trauma from one relationship and stop making what happened so personal. It had nothing to do with me. Infidelity happens, and while some couples survive, it's a reminder that I can overcome hard things without hardening for new relationships. And I am, in fact, the Beyonce of my hometown. *flips hair*

You can take credit for his glow-up, hygiene, calling his mother more often, you name it, but never for him being a dumbass. If he wants to, nothing (not even a billion dollars on an elevator) will stop him.

*Hector Hint: The post-elevator Solange incident refers to the infamous elevator fight between Beyonce's badass sister Solange and husband Jay-Z following an afterparty at the 2014 Met Gala. One can assume it was about him cheating, but this was before her Lemonade album dropped, in which she revealed their marriage had infidelity.

I hate hearing how much of a catch I am. Throw my ass back in the water if you're not going to stuff and admire me from your favorite wall.

Chapter Two:

SINGLE AF.

Driving the streets, backroads and
avenues of dating

SINGLE AF: The streets, backroads and avenues.

"If you fall in love, does your book turn into a romance novel?"

As a child of divorced parents, my examples of love in relationships were what I saw on TV through fictional characters and written storylines. I never got the "No boyfriends until you're 16" conversations or even the embarrassing chaperoned dates to make sure nothing fishy was happening. You meet the love of your life in high school, take matching photos together at the mall, get married, and have a baby.

I started dating my now ex-husband at 18 and was married by 26. So, the window of meeting a guy because I was hungry or simply making out for free drinks was not a thing. Instead of making mistakes and chasing my dreams, I focused on checking the boxes on life expectations. I'd never even had a fling or one-night stand. So, fast forward to 29, I'm only checking the "single" box on my taxes.

Following the implosion of Myspace and being too old to find someone walking around the mall, I had to do more than just exist to find someone new. A lot changed since the last time I dated. I no longer used my RAZR flip phone with the Nina Sky ring tone of "Move Ya Body" and I'm certain my Black Planet page as "Miss Mamacita" dissolved somewhere deep within the innerwebs. I'd already been married, so did I get a cheat sheet? Did I have to wait in line for the rest of the divorcees to wash up at a restaurant bar like everyone else? I'll order my Ruby Rita and happy hour loaded potato skins while I wait.

I'm in the streets in the form of online, and sometimes organic, dating for now. The convenience of meeting new people without sucking it in or doing your hair seemed easy enough, so I made a profile and I've been swiping. Frankly, it felt like Bourbon Street the morning after Mardi Gras. A lot of trash, drunk men giving compliments, and the aromatics of lingering fried food. Everyone's friendly, especially the men who can't read body language, and I end up barefoot, hungover, and wishing to be home. I've heard about the streets but never the backroads and avenues of dating cues, the odd feeling after having sex with a stranger, or playing off a sneeze fart during morning cuddles.

Being single as fuck has been a very insular experience, but I'm giving myself the grace to know the connection I'm craving is universal. It starts in the womb. Ironically, all I want to do now is lay in the fetal position and have my mother feed me.

Luckily I still have my old Forever 21 shirts, early 2000s booties, and worn ripped jeans for nights of side hugs in hopes of a meaningful connection.

So, online dating.

Dating has Plenty of Fish in th sea,
but there's just so much pee.

If online dating apps had honest descriptions and aptitude test requirements before downloading, I could've avoided a lot of heartache and headache. At one point, I was trying a new dating app every 30 days, and while I won't hold my breath on the standardized testing, I can depend on my ability to read through the bullshit to give my own descriptions.

Shiver my Tinders.
Tinder is that one drunk girl in the bathroom at the club who constantly compliments your hair and asks you where you got your jeans. She has a good time, but after a certain point her friends get tired of holding her up while she grinds on that random guy that bought her drinks throughout the night. That is Tinder. Incredibly entertaining, but also embarrassingly never it. There is a high plethora of shirtless men to penis ratios which makes conversation starters quite interesting with endless swiping options. Be prepared to be ghosted by the semi-cool guys and expect most of the connections to be like their profile height: A LIE.

unHinged.
Hinge was boring. It's sold as the most successful app for finding love, but it's hard to find a partner with corporate-style conversations like "What do you do for work?" while trying to sound professional in all my messages. It's like swiping for a man on Indeed. Between the wedding

dance photos and voice notes debating pineapple on pizza, I couldn't find anyone who didn't take themselves so seriously. We love a profile with "Want to get to know me? Just Ask," and pictures from their off-roading trip in the desert. It's the same responses with the same five-second video of them at a gym with a Snapchat filter. It's hella dry. If you try Hinge, be prepared for water cooler conversations about your weekend, and know everyone you meet, for the most part, will be a corporate lateral move in love.

Also, Hinge has international matching, which is cool until you realize love in Italy is also gray sweatpants and gym pics but now with a language barrier. Also, from personal experience, being rejected from 4400 miles away does sting a little more.

Rumble in my Bumble.
Bumble is the high school reunion of the other apps, where all the fuck boys come from Tinder, assuming the girls are "different." The men are the same, it just requires more effort. Be prepared for all the cringe-swiping after seeing all the leftovers from Tinder you avoided. That one guy that ghosted you? He's there. That one awkward conversation that went awry? He's there as well. Surprise! We are still outside.

Bumble's different in that the woman has to start the conversation when matched. For me, that meant mocking most first interactions with "What's your snap?" or an awkward suggestion of seeing dem titties before any niceties. I assume most of the men on Bumble love to have the "women want to be equal, but also want chivalry" conversations after a couple of matches.

Facebook Dating

Stay away! It's the ten-year high school reunion you've been avoiding. You know everyone because it pulls from your set location, and nothing is more mortifying than matching with the balding guy who took your virginity at 16. It's giving small town, and I moved away for a reason.

For starters, I created an immediate left swipe list in preparation:
-no cats
        -no skinny jeans
        -no designer clothes, including belts or cross-body satchels
         -no gym pics
        -no shirtless pics
        -no fishing photos (Rule of thumb: If he's fishing, he is, in fact, a catfish.)

*Disclaimer: this is *my* list. You probably have things on your list that aren't on the top of my "put a baby in me" registry either.

Red flags of online dating profiles.

You've been warned!

If he has one-letter profile names like "L" or "C": **Sir, what else are you hiding besides the other letters in your name?**

If he is over the age of 49 on a free dating website with profile pictures from the living room couch, and his profile questions have one-word responses: **Respectfully, use that 401k money and take that ass to eHarmony or Our Time.**

If he doesn't specifically state he has children (or doesn't) on his profile: **He does. A whole litter.**

If he talks a lot about crypto or bitcoin: **NFT means "No Fucking Thank You."**

If his profile's usernames are "supaman" or "ibeinthatcoochie" instead of an actual name: **Who are you hiding from: warrants or your wife?**

If he has "other" or "entrepreneur" as an occupation: **He is, in fact, unemployed.**

If in every picture he's wearing sunglasses or a hat: **He's ugly without them.**

Anyone named "Decklin" or "Shecklin": **His parents clearly hate him. Why even try?**

If he wants to argue with you about pineapple on pizza: **The Italian in me will fight you.**

If he only has dirty mirror photos with him wearing sunglasses and a popped collar in 2022: **It's giving early 2000s.**

If YouTube is his only source of news and entertainment, and he pays for it: **I need you to sign out immediately.**

If his car is clean, but his house is dirty: **His priorities are shit.**

If he complains about the time it takes you to reply, for example: "Why did you match me if you aren't going to respond, sweetie?": **Unmatch and dispatch.**

If the last book he read was The Hunger Games: **He can't read.**

If you go to his house and he has the Bravo app or Housewives: **He has a girlfriend, and she has impeccable taste in television.**

If he asks how much the appetizer or entrée was that you ordered: **Get your Cash App ready.**

Listen, when I get a tan, do my hair consistently, start eating properly, get another tan (this skin is translucent), brush my teeth every night (to include floss), learn to cook and season more than eggs, remember to apply deodorant after a shower, and not giggle when I'm uncomfortable at funerals: IT IS OVER FOR YOU BITCHES! AT THAT POINT, HIDE YOUR FATHERS AND FINE-ASS UNCLES.

Also, GMO Certified: Organic dating.

Just like this booty, I'm looking for something natural.

Speed Dating.
I had the idea of speed dating for a long time and finally built up the courage to try it. Yep, I bit the bullet and paid money to meet men. I found an event online and talked my homegirl into joining me. You can find many speed dating events with a simple Google search. This one cost $30, came with a free drink, and brought in multiple men between the ages of 26-39. I was hoping all the men would be older, but I was open to anything.

I went to the second floor of the building and immediately headed to the bar. A band practiced, so the awkward tension was cut with "Don't Stop Believin'" by Journey. It was just like the movies, the room full of people with many tables lined up against the wall, but only with bald men who avoided contact. After about 30 minutes of drinking and checking my phone, the host showed up and gave us cards to write down our favorites at the end. Every conversation was five minutes per person and, at the end, a bell would ring to move to the next person.

My first match was very high energy and had the biggest veneers I'd ever seen. He sat down, introduced himself, and the vibe was giving Funcle* (fun uncle) almost immediately. I was nervous and asked the most generic questions like "What do you do for fun?" to run out the clock. Between the music blaring and the lackluster conversation, once the bell rang, I was ready for another drink.

The rest of the night included close talking and awkward interactions. I remember one particularly because he resembled my father and had the gaze of a lion eyeing an antelope. I was the antelope. He was a photographer in the area and liked to reiterate that he had just bought a home. I could smell the captain and coke on his breath, with a hint of hot pocket for dinner. He sat closer to me and asked me for my Instagram. Can you imagine having a man who looks like your father with the breath of a whole pack of hotdogs in your face asking you about a username for an app he just learned how to use? Unbothered, I nodded like he said something else and sipped my soda water and lime. I held my breath for those five minutes waiting for my lungs to be relieved. After a handful of dates, everyone listed their top five out of ten, and we'd find out our matches within the next 24 hours. I got my matches through email and, before you ask, I never reached out.

Speed dating was entertaining but bring a friend. It's very awkward to intentionally meet someone in this type of setting and bringing someone relieved some of the nervousness. Be prepared. There's a type of man that signs up for speed dating. They're looking for wives or that-night hook-ups, but not much in between. On a positive note, it allowed me to talk to people I would never consider. It forced me to find a connection through conversation. The hardest part was not finding a connection of attraction and maintaining an in-depth conversation about Harry Potter until they called time.

The overall experience was great. Would I do it again? Only for free.

When trying to find love, get a little creative. Be open to going to unconventional settings to meet new people. It can be nerve-wracking to think about putting yourself out there, but the reward is knowing you are capable of doing different things. If you are too nervous, instead of saying it's something you could never do, bring a friend along for the great stories and experience.

Join a Co-ed League.

Shout out to the Boys & Girls Club basketball league for making me the most mediocre player with the confidence of Jordan in the 80s and 90s. If I had a dollar for every time I was passed a basketball in my life, I'd have $4. Knowing my skills were below beginner, I joined a co-ed basketball league with a good friend. I never met anyone. Three seasons in, the only thing getting action is my jump shot.

Joining a co-ed league is another non-conventional setting to meet active and competitive adults. Unfortunately, that competitiveness can get out of hand, but you can also rotate teams every season if the men are ugly (joking, but I am on my third team).

The Trader Joe's/Wegman's Effort.

Taking the idea of meet/cute** seriously, I'd dress up in my cutest leggings and go grocery shopping. My main character energy*** shined while picking out strawberries and reaching for the creamer on the top shelf at my big girl height of 5'2, making eye contact with strangers assuming they were obsessed with me.

To mix it up, I'd go to different groceries to see if the pool of potential lovers was different. Trader Joe's was the go-to place for the good-looking men from the gym. Giant had a lot of unbothered fathers, and Wegman's brought a mixture of good-looking single men who liked to cook, and good-looking women looking for those same men. I knew I needed to step my game up and throw on a little gloss when I saw they had restaurants and that wall of cheese selections. Find opportunities to feel good about yourself outside of the club or a night out. The grocery experience is practical because everybody eats. Also, you can tell a lot about a man by the food he buys. Disregard my $50 in snacks and that spinach – it'll be thrown away in a week after making my refrigerator smell like bitter grass.

Walk around Walmart.
A man will always bother you in Walmart, either for your number or a dollar.

For him to find you, you have to go outside.

*Hector Hint: A Funcle is the uncle that drinks too much at the family function, outstays his welcome and gets a little handsy and flirtatious with your friends.

**Hector Hint: A meet/cute is when two people go for the last rotisserie chicken at Costco and flustered, she says, "You can have it," as she tucks her thick and gorgeous "messy" hair behind her ear. It's a cliché interaction between two strangers that leads to either a relationship or a year of telling your friends you met the man of your dreams one year ago pumping gas.

***Hector Hint: Main character energy is any main character in your favorite movie who embodies the confidence and charisma that leads as a protagonist in the storyline. It's the girl who walks into a room and the music plays, fans blow, and everyone stops to stare. The popular jock that everyone knows, or the dog that saves the day. I know, far-fetched.

Learning "The Game."

Like any sport, there are rules.

After a successful first date, I'd rush home to call my girlfriends with the play-by-play. It'd take it from the top and explain every detail, from what he wore and ordered for dinner to what side of the sidewalk he walked on and if we held hands. It's amazing I'd be able to describe an evening of romance by the minute yet had to call my own mother to reconfirm my age, assuming I was 33: I'm 34.

So, imagine the confusion when I'd hear, "You can't text first," "You have to wait!" as a response to my excitement. Unaware at the time, this was playing the game.

I'm not athletic. I know you might be thinking, "Nik, not athletic? That's crazy." But playing a sport will forever humble me. Some people find it extremely easy to take up a sport, and for the most part, they will tell you in the process, "Yeah, I've played soccer since college," or, "I haven't played since middle school, but I can try." As for me, after two seasons playing volunteer point guard at the Boys and Girls Club, and three in an adult co-ed basketball league that's never won a game, you could call me Bleachers since that's where I always am.

Like sports, *playing the game of love* is like an actual game when you consider the following:

- Roster: Multiple prospects that are ranked by nicknames of their icks* from best to worst.
- Coach: YOU. Always in charge.
- Sideline Coaches: Your best friends who make suggestions, nicknames, notes, and reminders of why someone is benched.
- The Field: Where all your prospects battle for the opportunity to be picked.
- The Basket, Goal, Touchdown, etc.: Your vagina or heart, depending on the day.
- The Score: A list of their red flags.

And when I actually get to play, I saunter back and forth frantically asking my teammates, "Where do I go?" hoping no one will actually ask me to do anything or pass the ball. Similarly, I play the game of love frantic and lost.

If you aren't aware of the rules, let me give you some of the basics:

1. Never double-text.
> 2. Let them reach out to you first!
> 3. Don't overshare!
> 4. Don't be forward.
> 5. Immediately set boundaries.
> 6. Don't be too available.

And the list goes on.

As expected, these new-found rules did not come easy. I broke them, and I still break them, over the last six years as I've been dating or in relationships. Aside from not being well-versed in the playbook, they also were the complete opposite of my natural being. I'm too open, easily excited, and enjoy making future plans, the absolute bane of the game.

Shout out to the women who play the game, build a roster of men to entertain and leave them wanting more. I commend you. I tried to go on many dates and text multiple men throughout the day but couldn't do it. I barely remember what I ate in a day, so having the same conversation with three different men felt like a full-time job with no PTO or benefits.

The rules started to ruin my experience of meeting a new person. They were so specific and not at all subjective. I started to second-guess everything. "Do I say this? Does this sound okay? Is it too soon?" I could no longer make my own decisions based on feelings and excitement. It didn't matter if I liked him or the vibes were right, I had to follow these social media-enforced requirements. It became more stressful and less fun. I was writing people off quickly and questioning the results after a couple of months. I'd do what others told me to do and end up disappointed and defensive that another opportunity ended after doing everything others suggested. While helpful in setting limits and slowing down the process of getting to know someone, it added too much pressure to finding the right person.

I needed to create my own set of rules based on what I wanted. They were specific to how I felt from my experiences, instead of what I was told from a TikTok, supportive friend, or relationship podcast. I made them specific to my gut feelings and emphasized some things that immediately turned me off in the beginning.

When I double-text, how do I feel?
> 1. How does this person make me feel physically?
> 2. Does he say "calm down" or "relax" often?
> 3. Is he moving too fast on the first date?
> 4. Is he consistent?

Ways to create your own rules:

You are the master of things that bother you. Create rules that you can hold as a baseline for any new relationship. Remember these rules are specific to you and what you need. It normally takes a little longer to meet a person you connect with, but having an idea of your expectations before you get into something more serious can help you moving forward before it's too late. Once people show you their true colors, and if it happens to be puke green, read the signs, and move accordingly.

For example: I hate first dates where the guy immediately talks about sex. Not only is it definitely not happening, but it also says so much about a person willing to talk about his favorite position and kinks to a stranger. I could know your mother!

Know your non-negotiables. Write down the things you're not willing to compromise on and stick to them. Nothing is too big or too small if it is something you value. Don't forget you are doing the picking. While the distractions come in the form of beautiful, emotionally unavailable men, it's a waste of time. Unless it's Michael B. Jordan, then change them all to whatever he wants. Just playing (kind of). But make a list and check it often. Check it often to revisit your choices. Reflection on your experiences will change your mentality.

I'm hopeful one day to retire from the game and be on the sidelines cheering for the free agents. I'd reminisce and rub my knees from all the years of playing full court. The good ol' days when I'd go to the club and men yelled at me, "Dat ass phat" or those who'd "call me tomorrow" without ever hearing from them again. Until then, it's nothing but assists and airballs.

Create your own rules like Uno.

*Hector Hint: "icks", *pronounced /ik/*, are the unromantic, unattractive things your partner unwillingly does that either gross you out or remind you how even the most beautiful, "perfect" person is still human. "Icks" can be how they chew, the way they speak to their mother, that one lazy eye that appears when they laugh, how often they brush their teeth, or even their lack of ambition. Some of my personal icks have ranged from the way they scratch their back to using the word "supposably" instead of "supposedly."

Diversify your portfolio.

References upon request.

When using the apps, I'd always swipe on the same type of guy. Big beard, hearty, wore flannel, tattoos, and some type of expensive sneakers. You don't need to say it, I will: fuck boy. Shockingly they all acted, reacted, and interacted the same from the swipe right to dinner. It was disheartening and monotonous. So, treating these dates like the stock market, I started to diversify my dating portfolio with different men outside my "type." I expanded my age range, changed interests and even religious affiliations, hoping to mix up the ideals, lifestyles, and vibes of the monotony of dating. Like any healthy portfolio, my experiences will reduce the risk of disappointment through a range of emotional and physical investments.

Types of Diversifying Options:
- Date ugly; you *know* what's ugly to you.
- Try someone who can't answer where they were on January 6th.
- Date broke.
- Date that one guy who drinks whole milk or Dr. Pepper 6 am at the office.
- Try the guy who records TikTok dances in public.
- Date a PC or Dell user.

Please refer to the successful people who decided to try something new and ended up with someone they never expected yet it just worked. Trying new dating experiences only adds better opportunities for my next relationship. With a certification in "fuck boy-ism" or training in "how to deal with a narcissist," my list of expertise makes me well-versed and prepared for my next position as girlfriend.

...and after taking my own advice, now a retraction.

I like to keep it honest all the time, and, for months, I've actively taken my own advice of dating blindly, which leads to this retraction and a better understanding of why the friend zone exists. Every new guy was so kind, funny, and intelligent, but by the end of the night, I dreaded the walk to the car with a chance of a kiss. I tried but could not see myself having sex with any of them. Not saying the possibility could never change, but – unless you look like Matthew McConaughey and show up chiseled in a snug white t-shirt after working all day on the ranch, looking for a glass of water, and a woman's house to fix – it wasn't happening honey.

Instead of looks, be open to diversifying personality traits, responsibilities, and moral compass in a person because attraction is a game changer when it comes to dating. We want that excitement, a reason to put on concealer, and someone that, frankly, gets us wet. THERE! I said it. We've all given an ugly a chance, until he blocks you after seeing your feet. Yes, ugly is subjective, but we all have a type, and it's okay to admit it. Instead of the usual, try someone who doesn't drink, prays outside of needing something, or volunteers in his spare time.

The energy was there, but unfortunately, my vagina was not.

From the Book of Boy Fuckery: Common dating translations

Squint eyes, bites lip.

"I'm not a good person."
He means it, and yes, that is trauma speaking.

"I'm not looking for anything serious."
No, his mind won't change for you.

"I'm open to the idea…" (when talking about a relationship/children/ marriage)
He's open to it with one specific person that is not you.

"My job gets very busy."
Girl, he works from home at a damn standing desk in the spare bedroom. He doesn't want to talk to you.

"I'll give you a call tomorrow."
It's 3 pm on a Tuesday. Read the room, baby.

"I'm looking for someone that's emotionally intelligent."
He wants you to put up with his temper tantrums.

"My moon sign is in Leo."
He heard that from another woman and he says it because he thinks it makes him more interesting.

"I have a 1-year-old."
He's still in a relationship with his child's mother. No, she doesn't know he's texting you.

"I have a couple of friends."
These friends are only from his job, and they can't stand his ass for real, for real.

"Okay, Calm Down!"
Be prepared to hear that anytime you have an opinion or disagree with him.

"She's not someone you need to worry about."
Be worried about her.

"Sure."
He doesn't want to do it.

"I normally don't do this, but for you, I'll try."
He literally does it for everyone.

"I'm emotionally available and only looking for long-term commitment."
He will waste your time.

"I'm done with the games."
He means Xbox, not your potential relationship.

"I have many jobs."
He doesn't have a job.

Rubs hands, "So what's your body count?"

The advancement of technology in the 21st century has allowed us to live in the time of Chat GPT, the James Webb Space Telescope, and the advancement of gene sequencing, and you want to know my favorite color? The only colors I know are red flags, blue balls, Yellow fever, red dye 40, and silver linings.

Chapter Three:

MINGLE.

The lessons from dating debauchery,
in no particular order.

MINGLE: Pour a little out for the blocked homies.

In Memoriam:
Cue Sarah McLachlan's "Angel" instrumental (that one commercial with the homeless puppies).

Ahem, I wanted to take a moment to thank all the men of my dating past for all the things they've taught me. I hope you find freedom in knowing every weird interaction, awkward first kiss, or unsolicited sext has made me exhausted and unhopeful that good men ever roamed this earth aside from Jesus himself.

The time we took to figure out what we hated about each other wasn't terrible, and that included the sex. It needs to be stated (since every woman with an opinion about a man is deemed as a feminist troll who hates masculinity), I don't hate you. You're the reason I can say to myself, "Shit, at least I'm not so and so." And if you wonder if it's you, it is. I've appreciated our time together, and while every encounter led closer to our demise, I learned so much about myself.

Your projections built me up to see my superpower. For the longest, I thought it was you who brought the sunshine, but it was me. You're right; I am "too much" and "a lot to handle," and when you made me feel small or contain my puppy dog energy with a "calm down," it was a reminder of just how dope I was. Through your disappointments, I was able to leave with lessons that gave me a better understanding of my future in love. You've played a part in me getting closer to the love I deserve.

I've appreciated all the apologies through WhatsApp, emails, and handwritten letters. There will never be a chance of us ever getting back together, but I hope everyone is doing well on the other side of my blocked list.

"The person you are trying to reach is not accepting calls at this time. Please try your call again never."

*Please note: The following are all real stories from my dating past with names changed to eliminate the weird flex of bragging about being in a book, but mainly because my broke ass can't afford a lawyer.

Dating Lesson: When asking the universe for something, be specific.

The universe has a sense of humor.

I am a sucker for a "hey baby" text. There's something about a man being confident enough to start a conversation calling me "baby" that gets me giddy. It is such a red flag, but talking to someone who clearly knows how the game works and uses it to his advantage is a problem. Not for him, but for me.

I met "Mr. In and Out" and immediately noticed his confidence. A little older than me, he was very handsome with a raspy voice that'd make any indie singer jealous. His profile said he had a son and lived about an hour away. After a couple of days of texting back and forth online, we ended up exchanging numbers and started talking pretty often. I'd get a "hey baby" or "come see me" text throughout the day, which made me smile. He said all the right things and gave me enough emotional attention for me to hang around. I knew this was never going anywhere, but the distraction of flirting and being playful with someone new was welcomed.

A couple of days later, we FaceTimed. Personally, I hate FaceTime "dates" since the initial interaction is awkward and there's no opportunity to look anywhere else but the camera. Imagine just being face to face with someone you just met, holding a conversation, and still leaving hungry. There's a reason why I never have my camera on Zoom meetings or use Omegle* for fun. It's all fun and games until you FaceTime a new match and see that one missing tooth in the front you didn't catch in any of his pictures, but I digress.

He looked a lot like his pictures (which is always a plus), but after talking for a while, it was the only authentic thing about him. He had multiple, MULTIPLE, children and a 10+ year relationship that he just recently got out of a couple of months ago. I tried not to react, but in true Nikki fashion, it was all over my face. His response to my shock was, "I'm a true Scorpio, what can I say?" as if the day he was born allowed him to hide the fact that he had children.

As the conversation continued, he asked "So, what are you looking for?" and my response of "a husband" quickly moved the conversation to an ending. The next morning my "good morning baby" texts turned into "wyd" around 2pm. I could tell from his text energy he clearly wasn't looking for the same thing, but I was happy it took no time to find out. He never planned a date or tried to really learn who I was, which is respectable. It was what it was, with no fluff or filler needed.

Fast forward to almost a year later. It's Valentine's Day and I'm dreading the overly-hyped holiday of chocolate and flowers as a desperately single person. I woke up melancholic, anticipating people at work talking about all their plans with their super attractive, caring, understanding boyfriends. Never the type to celebrate the holiday even when in a relationship, it was hitting me harder than usual that, after months of actively trying to find someone, it simply was not happening.

I normally have internal conversations with the universe, but that day, I asked her out loud, "Can you bring me someone to talk to, someone to spend time with?" during my lunch break. Maybe an hour or so later, I got a text from an unsaved number saying, "Hey, how are you?" with a hand-waving emoji. I responded with, "Who is this?" and started detective work as to who it was. I'd normally block all the men from my dating past, so this was unexpected. After a line of questioning Olivia Benson (Law & Order: SVU) would be proud of, I found out the mystery man was Mr. In and Out.

As if the universe was bored on the biggest manifesting holiday, she listened to me. She gave me exactly what I asked for in record time: a person to talk to and spend time with. But why him? Out of all people, him? This was not what I wanted! After a couple of texts, he started with the "come stay with me" talk as if the almost year of us not talking made me hornier. I politely declined and he was blocked to never spin "the block" again.

I couldn't help but laugh. Okay girl, you win. I'll sit my anxious ass right here. This was a lesson in knowing the power of asking and being specific. I needed specificity but asked for anything. The universe was like, "play stupid games, win stupid prizes" and I humbled myself immediately.

Meeting Mr. In and Out was a reminder that some of these men will blatantly lie and hide things to get the attention they want. They know they will never be able to give you what you want but will still try to waste your time. Most importantly, it's a reminder that when asking the universe for what you want, make sure you are specific. If not, she will send the bottom of the barrel as a test to see if you are really about that life, or just wasting her time.

The next time the universe answers your request with a random text from your past, do the following:

Don't take the bait.
This is a test to see if all the things you repost on social media about knowing yourself and your value are true.

Understand his "why."
He is bored and genuinely doesn't care how you've been. Unless he texts with a place to send flowers and a $1000 gift card to pay for a year of coffee, I'm not interested. Don't let people have access to you that had it and lost it. There's your reason why.

Don't believe the hype.
They haven't changed and nothing is different.

<u>Mr. In and Out</u>

Red Flags
It's giving Nick Cannon**.
Never planned a date.
Too comfortable, too fast.

Green Flags
Funny.
Sexy voice.
Successful.

*Hector Hint: Omegle is a free website where you can video chat with strangers. Be prepared for a lot of penises and creepers in undershirts.

**Hector Hint: Nick Cannon currently has 12 children with multiple women. Who knows how many he will have once this book is published.

Dating Lesson: Attraction doesn't mean good sex.

"No Ragrets."

I'm pretty comfortable in my sexuality but adding sex to dating has been a process. I've never had a one-night stand or even made out with a random at a bar after too many skinny girl margaritas. So, sex in my late 20s after being married was quite a doozy. Don't get me wrong, I be fuckin' (again, sorry parents), but getting to actual penetration was the most awkward for me.

This might come as a surprise, but I am not the smoothest. I squeal, tense up, blush, and do everything in my power to get over the first of anything. I hate the game of trying to make a move without acting like you're trying to make a move. I absolutely hate it. Now, of course, once the band-aids ripped off, it's just regular at that point, but I tend to rush the first physical interaction out of sheer embarrassment. Normally it happens around the third date if I see some form of longevity. Let's just get it over with already.

If you read the *Does This Divorce Make Me Look Fat?*, the "Infamous Fuck Boy" chapter talked about the finest man I met when living in NYC and, regrettably, I didn't have sex with him. When I met The Infamous Fuckboy 2.0 online, he had a similar build, attractiveness, tattoos, muscles, and, just like the first, a problem. I say a problem because that's the type of good-looking man that would have me picking up his kids from school, fighting random women in public, and cosigning a car loan before I knew it. We matched online and quickly clicked and exchanged numbers. I should've known he was going to be a chapter after sending me a video of him in bed with his arm behind his head, casually watching a movie while asking what I was doing, but I decided to play.

Unexpectedly, the conversation flowed with funny, light banter, and before I knew it, it was 3am and I was debating why The Office was better than Parks & Recreation through voice text. The next day, expecting not to hear much (per online dating fashion), 2.0 sent a good morning text and we chatted sporadically throughout the day. When we met up, he was even more attractive in person. I'm sure it was the energy from our spirited conversations, but dinner was good. I was super nervous, he noticed, and we laughed about it until dessert.

After dinner, we decided to go to a dive bar with free popcorn and seasonal beers. I felt a little less tense after chugging my first beer and pounding the popcorn like we didn't just eat our weight in family portions of pasta. At some point, he decided to take off his jacket and I noticed his tattoo poking from the corner of the neck of his t-shirt. That's when I knew I was going to have sex with this man no matter what the outcome was. My tatted redemption.

For context, the original infamous fuck boy was the first time I regretted not having sex with someone for the sheer fact that he was the finest man I'd met at that point in my life. It was the first time I started online dating before experiencing an actual fuck boy or dick pics, and he delivered both. We met, clicked, but he was open about just having fun. 2.0 seemed to want more.

I remember feeling my pussy throb watching his tattoo poke

out of his shirt from his collarbone. Side note: I know my best friend is dying as she reads this, but it had to be said. The night ended without a kiss, but with the promise of a second date. For a couple more weeks, we washed and repeated conversations about movies, shows, life experiences, and plans for second and third dates. My attraction was building, and after our third date, I was ready. The next night he asked to come by and watch a movie, to which I agreed. I was in track during high school, and I don't think I'd ever run faster to the bathroom to shave my entire body after that call.

It took over an hour to turn into a dolphin in human form. I slipped on some tighter, sexier lounge clothes. My plan was simple. Once he walked into the house, I'd prance around, we'd start making out, and quickly take things to the bedroom. When he texted that he was close, I sweat through my crème-colored t-shirt from the nerves. This was out of character for me to intentionally be extra sexy in hopes that it would lead to sex. I talk a lot of shit, but this was the one-pointer needed to win the game. I anticipated we'd get to it rather quickly, but once he got to my house I disappointingly lounged on the couch.

After a couple of hours of Netflix and absolutely no chill, he could sense my tension. My body language showed my overthinking and awkwardness. "You're being weird. What's up?" he said. I acted like nothing was happening while my mind was racing about how I could strategically be cool and sexy while sweating through yet another shirt. I sat there for a couple of moments before the word vomit spewed out, "I want to have sex with you!" We sat there in silence for a couple of minutes, and he looked over and said, "So, the bedroom?"

It was a mixture of excitement that it was actually happening and fear that it was actually happening, sprinkled with some playfulness and imposter syndrome. My inner track star ran to the bedroom, immediately undressed, and got into the bed. (Similar to that one scene in Bruce Almighty when he, Jim Carrey, undressed by putting his arms down, like that.) Assuming he got the "rip the band-aid off" sex memo, I looked up to him slowly taking off his clothes. As if that was an invitation to help, I got my hairless, lotioned, nervous, sweaty body up to undo his shirt and bracelet.

Thinking about it now, removing the bracelet was pointless. It had no purpose and, while an eye-sore to look at since it was one of those bracelets you get from a tropical island with beads, it got in the way of nothing. Also, I couldn't even get it off! Which made it even more embarrassing as I stood there naked and waiting for him to take off his bracelet before sex. IT WAS A FUCKING BRACELET!

Also, before you wonder, we used a condom. I'd be wondering too.

A few moments later, that was it. The sex was anti-climactic in more ways than one. Between multiple sex poses where I held in my farts to do pretzel or reverse cowgirl and the awkward bedroom talk, I was ready for it to be over. The bracelet took longer to get off than him. Fulfilling my tatted redemption meant bypassing values for looks, which was disappointing without feelings and sexual compatibility. I rushed the process and ended up twisted like Auntie Anne's, bloated with a man wearing a pookah shell necklace. So, while it was on the bucket list, it's noted that attraction is not a qualifier for great sex.

We ran our course after I had the dreaded, "What are we?" conversation that he couldn't answer.

Red Flags
Difficult accessories.
Bedroom talk was similar to Johnny Bravo (the cartoon).

Green Flags
Fine as fuck.
Great personality.

Dating Lesson: Weed em' out with diarrhea.

Shit happens, literally.

Flakey people are a marker of online dating. I've met a lot of men who seemingly were interested, started making plans for dinner or drinks, and never heard from them again. I met a guy online who wasn't around long enough to get a nickname but piqued my interest with his very entertaining and responsive text game. He was a bit nerdy, and different than what I'd experienced in regard to conversation from online dating. We'd talk for most of the day until a certain point where he'd ghost me and reappear the next morning with an excuse as to why he stopped responding. Assuming the normal battle rhythm, I simply asked, "Did you have diarrhea?" to his silence. He responded with a laughing emoji and never responded again.

Aside from it being funny, his no response was a response for how he'd take to my humor and personality in the future. I tend to hold off on the inappropriate jokes until after the third or fourth date. This goes without saying, but as the leader of the "things you shouldn't say" club, I am very open about everything (hence two books about everything from moving to a new city to learning I had a third hole). The benefit of him going quiet after a mild joke was that it expedited the process of learning if someone had a similar sense of humor, or the patience to deal with my antics. Weeding him out with diarrhea talk eliminated the "you shouldn't curse as a woman" or the "Ew, periods? That's disgusting" type of guys. For those who find diarrhea a bit too risqué, I'd suggest volleying a mild fart or herpes joke.

Other ways to weed them out with diarrhea include:

Be effortlessly you.
Talk in TikTok references, do that one baby voice that comes out when you drink too much wine, do the choreography to "Single Ladies," show that specific talent of playing "Ode to Joy" on the recorder, brag about getting a bingo that one night at the VFW, and talk about Harry Potter. The quirky things about you are what makes you great, don't change that shit.

Women are funnier, and men need to accept it already.
Crack those jokes, and don't hold back on the side comments. We are fucking funny, and seeing how a person you're talking to handles that is vital. Coming from personal experience, the way someone reacts to the loud and spirited energy I bring into a room says a lot about them. If who I am makes you uncomfortable, respectfully fuck off.

Remind yourself sometimes it has nothing to do with you and more to do with your bathroom humor. Allow people to make the decision if they want to stay around or not.

While embarrassing, his decision to never respond was probably for the best, seeing the fact that when I'm really secure, I fart a lot and blame it on the dog.

Dating Lesson: Someone's comfort is a gift.

Sir, your insecurities are showing.

In my improv class, we learned about the benefit of *gift-giving*. It's essentially the idea that whatever someone gives you is used as a tool to move a scene along. It can be an object, idea, physical characteristic, or even a relationship. In dating, how a person talks and treats you when they're comfortable can also be a gift. I'm not referring to how they sleep with a CPAP due to sleep apnea, I'm talking about the slight jabs or comments said in a joking manner at your expense. A gift is a piece of information that can give more insight into who they are or how they perceive you.

It's not uncommon working in comedy for people to either hate the fact I make people laugh or appreciate it. I've heard jokes at my expense, comments about things I can't control, or blatant lies in an attempt to show how funny I'm not. Not to mention the ones that want me to prove my funniness by telling them a joke, to which I respond, "Pay me first." I've experienced it often as a funny person. I'm loud, inappropriate, sometimes obtuse, and easily excited. Some of the men I've dated have used it to tear me down, highlighting my shortcomings and hitting below the belt.

I've heard the following from men I've dated:
"You run into rooms instead of walking."
"You're embarrassing."
"You aren't even that funny."
"Aren't nose rings a little trashy?"
"You're so obnoxious."

It's definitely hurtful and, as a naturally defensive person, I could've immediately made a joke about them lying about their height or how they're prematurely balding but, instead, I've accepted the gift of how they viewed me once they felt more secure. It can be sold in a flippant, light manner, but it's how they saw me. Similarly to a drunk person speaking a sober person's mind, the gift of someone's ability to tear you down is a glimpse into your future. Just imagine when they know about your vulnerabilities and secrets. When someone gets too comfortable and says mean or slick comments at the expense of you early into meeting, you take that gift and return it.

Your ability to be intelligent, independent, and successful is intimidating to insecure men. Fortunately for you, through their ingrained patriarchal habits, they will quickly show you their intimidation with their commentary. Don't assume everyone who treats you nicely is in your corner. To many, you're empowering and influential, and to others, you're a threat to their own limitations.

Not a Lesson: A perfect first date.

Picture this: You meet a guy online and, as the conversation flows, he asks if you're available within the next week to have dinner. Excited for the opportunity to meet someone new, you send him your availability with a couple of dates and, soon after, you receive an email confirmation for a Saturday reservation. It's at a new French restaurant not too far from your house that you mentioned earlier in the conversation and the time takes into consideration your work schedule, so you won't have to rush. The date is set, and phone numbers are exchanged.

Every morning, you hear from him, and, on the day of the date, he texts you first about the date and says he can't wait to see you in person. Throughout the day, you chat here and there and the vibes are immaculate. The workday ends and, on your way home, he texts you the dress code and asks if you'd like him to pick you up or send an Uber. Uncomfortable with a stranger knowing where you live, you let him send you money for an Uber and get ready.

The clock strikes 7pm and an Uber Black pulls up with a gentleman getting out of the car to open the door. His name is Michael, and he's very professional. Once you get in, you get a text about your date being early to the restaurant and he'll wait for you before getting the table.

Once you arrive at the restaurant, Michael opens the door

and you can see him standing at the door, holding flowers, excited to see you. You embrace and soon after are seated at the best table in the restaurant. The menu is prefixed based on the chef's recommendations, and he orders a bottle of Pinot Noir – another thing you casually mentioned liking before that he remembered. The rest of the evening you talk about love languages, each other's goals and funny quirks that end up being similarities while eating delicious French cuisine. At the end of the night, the server drops off the check and the head chef stops by to say hello. You watch as he talks to the chef like an old friend: confident, funny, and poised. After introductions are made, he looks at the check without hesitation and pays as the chef leaves to finish up the dinner rush.

After dinner is over, he gets up to help you from your seat and assists with your jacket. Grabbing your hand to lead you to the front, he walks with you through a crowd of people, never letting you go. Once you get to the front, excited for whatever's next, you see the Uber Black and Michael patiently waiting to take you home. "This was a lovely evening and I'd love to do this again soon," he says. You smile and agree with a hug in hopes a last-minute kiss is available, which it isn't. He kisses you on the cheek and opens the door, "Let me know when you get home." You get in and watch him waiting until you turn the street toward your home.

Almost home, you get a text notification and it's him. "Tonight was absolutely amazing, and you are stunning. I can't wait to see you again." You smile contagiously at your phone, waiting to respond when you get in. You get home safely, respond, and immediately call your best friend to give every intricate detail of your evening: from wearing the worst heels that make your booty pop to how good his cologne smelled. She's been by the phone all night, patiently waiting to hear the after-action report with popcorn in hand.

After getting through the initial excitement of a successful date, you immediately say, "This is my husband," and now you're picking out flowers, place settings, and color schemes for this man. I'll let you savor this fantasy before I get in that ass, but I'm here to remind you: this is NOT the Bachelor, Love is Blind, or 90 Day Fiancé. First Dates are a facade.

Dating Lesson: First dates are a facade.

Not everything is a meet/cute.
You might just really have food in your teeth.

I've had terrible interviews, auditions, or even bad Mexican food (which is hard to conceive), but when it comes to first dates, I've been lucky. The plans set with minimal questions, the restaurants of all my favorite foods, and the conversations would flow like the bottle of Pinot Noir ordered for the table.

Some first dates were so magical that I'd get so caught up in the immediate chemistry and vulnerability of the person that I'd ask myself if it were love at first sight. I met the mother fucker on Tinder, and our first date was out of a Taylor Swift song. I mean, we ended the night eating ice cream on his truck bed, laughing about shit that didn't matter. It was a different type of energy and enthusiasm that I wasn't expecting.

I called him the mother fucker since he told me a story about having sex with a girl in college and her mother soon after. YES! Definitely a red flag, but I disregarded all the flags, signs, and smoke signals since he was funny, consistent, and wanted me. He'd remember the small things, surprise me with flowers every time we met, and make the time to drive over an hour for just an hour of my time. I gave him the blueprint and he followed it. So, imagine my surprise when plans for a second date started to get pushed farther and farther into the future.

We'd meet in the middle for conversation in cars and would go to each other's houses for more conversations and take-out dinners. The idea of another magical first date was quickly forgotten as we slipped into comfort very fast without knowing one another. After month two of doing the same monotonous things, the things that once attracted me to the mother fucker, were slowly leaving. He stopped dressing up, buying flowers, or even paying for dinner. I was playing house with a bum.

Not to mention the disrespect. I'd notice a random hairclip, flowers, and, one time, a cake when I went to his house. I emphasize the cake because bitches bake cakes. It was a box mix in an aluminum foil tray; I remember.

I called them "second date strangers" since the second date would normally look like going Dutch on a Denny's Grand Slam: dull conversations and all the niceties out the window. This wasn't the first time this happened, and I quickly learned about the first date representative.

Similar to a company's customer service, the representative is the person who represents the company on a recorded line, a spokesperson of sorts. They're extremely professional and patient, and most importantly, do things for the best interest of the company. In this case, the first date representative was vested in my attention. If I had a sentence, he'd finish it. An issue, he'd fix it! He hated online dating because no one wanted monogamous relationships anymore. He was calculated to like what I liked and wanted for everything I wanted. In this case, I wanted a relationship with the mother fucker's representative, and his ass was on a lunch break for months. There's a possibility that this person's intentions were genuine and sincere, but it seemed like this was only offered temporarily to satisfy his immediate physical, mental, or emotional needs.

I begged him to give me more, and in response, he said, "You're asking for too much!" It was embarrassing how often I asked him to change instead of accepting this was the best it was going to get. I became exhausted from the inconsistencies and emotions. After months of watching Law & Order SVU episodes on his couch, and him "forgetting" his wallet too many times, we broke up over him not paying for a Chipotle bowl of barbacoa. I knew a relationship with him would cost me in more ways than one if we were beefing over $14.

The next time you find yourself confused, consider the following:

Look at every date as an interview: Think like you're corporate and he's a fresh out of college graduate. He'll show up with a resume, tailored suit, and a list of follow-up questions in preparation for the job (you). But there's a reason why there are multiple rounds of interviews. You don't want to rush the process and end up teaching him how to make a copy. If you feel like things are inauthentic, it's because they are. Take your time in the process of making a choice and you'll be able to see if the skillset matches the person.

Date more than one person at a time: Try to keep the roster full, or at least keep someone on the side so you're not putting all your uterus eggs in one basket. Consistency is the name of the game, and options make it easier for you not to immediately dote over the little things that come with good manners.

Almost everything is game: He's probably talking to other people. Instead of worrying about what that means for you, enjoy the show-and-tell at Friday dinner with the girls.

Answer the question, "Do I even like them?": It's easy to get carried away when someone's being nice to you (especially if it's been a while), but figure out if you even like him, and what you want before drinking your delusional cocktail. If you can't answer the question without being superficial, they can't either.

There's a reason why my first dates are so magical. It's because the representative is energized to waste the time of someone new. If his behavior changed after a night of opening the car doors, dinner, and great conversation; if once the clock turns midnight, those jeans turn bleached and torn, his vocabulary changes from "sure, let me plan something" to "you tell me," and his phone is always on "Do not disturb," press 0 for a manager. Enjoy the opportunity to meet a new person but remember a first impression doesn't always show a person's true character.

Dating Lesson: Ghosting doesn't have to be scary.

A graveyard of text messages.

I can't speak for all millennials, but the *ghosters* of my time were moms. If someone called that we wanted to avoid, they'd simply give a "She can't come to the phone right now," or would interrupt the landline and say they needed to get on the internet.

Nowadays, ghosting* seems to be a way to avoid our problems. We ghost meetings, people, and sometimes even bills. Yet, those fuckers find us every time. I remember the first time I was ghosted: The date was fine, no hiccups, and I was on my best behavior (i.e., ordered only one appetizer, didn't ask who he voted for, or make a joke about his mother), so to hear nothing after or the next day was unexpected. Not even a "sorry, not sorry" or a "cool" followed with a presumably green bubble. Nothing.

Without explanation, I started to spiral. Was it something trivial like breath? Or how I responded to the 21-questions game? Was it my affinity for watching pimple-popping videos? The verdict was out and no amount of garlic breath or TV preferences mattered. I had been left on eternal "Delivered."

In the days after, I kept rereading the text chain looking for awkward moments, blips, or burps that might've made sense for why he didn't reach out. I had to accept I was never going to get that answer. My range of emotions went from the initial disappointment of the potential relationship to the ego hit that it actually happened. I wrecked my brain until I found the silver lining that getting ghosted was the answer. It saved the time of getting to know a new person that didn't want a future with me, but also gave clarity on a person's emotional intelligence and maturity. The decision was already made, and no number of conversations or clarifications was going to change that. Instead of trying to figure out what I did wrong, it had nothing to do with me.

I normally always put the blame on myself whenever something goes wrong in love. What did I do and how could I have avoided it? I put the burden on myself to find a solution, thinking this slightly balding man might be flawed in spotting a bad bitch. Of course, I'm able to eloquently convey when I'm not interested, but who knows why this man couldn't. I had to stop giving this person who I spent two hours with the benefit of the doubt. At the end of the day, a person's disinterest in you is a loss for them, point blank, period. Instead of wrecking your brain about why he ghosted you, find his dad on Facebook and fuck him out of spite.

Ghosting tells you the type of person you were going to potentially deal with and eliminates the headache of that person in the future.

*Hector Hint: Ghosting is when someone stops responding without warning, leaving the other person to assume it was something they did, said, or smelled like.

Dating Lesson: The retraction to "Diversify your portfolio".

Some rules are meant to be broken.

After multiple years of first dates, I've created an internal checklist for the sake of my safety and sanity.

1. Never kiss on the first date. The lean-in face right before a kiss is an ick from a stranger. *Please see my full list of icks on page 99

2. Give it at least two dates before ending the connection. Second dates can show you a lot after meeting the representative.

3. Offer to pay half for the first date and if he lets you, he's cheap.

4. If sex is a topic of conversation at any point on the first date, there won't be a second.

5. Extra points if they offer to come pick you up, but never let them since violence against women happens way more often than we think. Fuckers.

But like all rules, you forget why they were created and have to break them from time to time. I met The Update, and the only thing that piqued my interest was the first date free meal. Before the date, we FaceTimed, and I immediately knew he was not for me. He gave off the "I'm too cool to get to know someone" vibe with a flirty but antagonizing demeanor. I just remember he'd have a sarcastic response to everything I said. For example, I say something like, "I love art exhibits," to which he'd respond with, "Yeah, okay," as he rubbed his hands and licked his lips. Needless to say, it was awkward for the 20 minutes we were on the phone.

Assuming he'd sense my disinterest, I was surprised to get a follow-up text asking about my availability for the week ahead and plans to go to an art exhibit. I wasn't interested, but respectful of my rules and my willingness to try anything at this point, I decided to go.

Our first date was a couple of days later at an art exhibit in the city. I was late due to parking, and he was on time and dressed for what seemed like an interview: a dress shirt and slacks. I was quite the opposite, dressed like an interviewee for a job they didn't want: jeans and a t-shirt from the thrift store. He seemed excited to see me, which was appreciated, and I repeatedly apologized for being underdressed to which he responded with, "You look great."

Over the next couple of hours, we walked around the exhibit and talked while watching ceiling projections of flowers in different forms. I started to notice him getting more comfortable with our conversation, but the chemistry was still not prevalent. I kept telling myself to give it a chance, be open, see what happens, and after a couple more hours of talking over tacos, we called it a night. I left with an appreciation for seeing the date through, but knowing this was the end of us. Before I could muster up the courage to have the "it's you, not me" conversation, he messaged me with another date planned for the weekend. I knew there was no chemistry or attraction, but as a stickler for the rules, I decided to give it one last try. I chopped it up to first date jitters or the tightness of his slacks cutting off oxygen to his brain.

The next date was at a Thai restaurant, and this time he was late, over 30 minutes to be exact, with no communication or explanation. His response to my call was a nonchalant, "I'm about to be there," as if I had no reason to be annoyed. I ordered a glass of wine and gave him five more minutes, the time it took for me to finish my drink. He arrived five minutes after that, unapologetic. I ordered another glass of wine and prepared for our last supper.

I don't think I'd eaten Pad Thai faster in my life. The energy was off. His conversation was sarcastic and a bit cockier since the first date. I felt disrespected by his side comments and sly remarks as if he was doing me a favor by being there, and his lack of consideration was something that should not be accepted. My rules backfired for The Update, knowing I didn't want a relationship, and now I was waiting at a hole-in-the-wall Thai restaurant for my carry-out box and the check.

Once he paid, I bolted to my car, dreading the thought of him trying to kiss me goodbye. He had a way of not picking up on social cues, and while I was on the verge of telling him about his hairline, it wasn't in me to be mean when I knew this was never happening again. He walked me to my car (I parked in the front), and I left. Not one to ghost, The Update was never going to hear from me again.

A week later, I got a "What happened to you?" text, to which I replied, "Respectfully, I'm good."

I created my rules thinking they would help me find a partner without considering that some of these people are undeserving. The catastrophe of The Update showed me that my time and energy are finite. Someone showing

interest doesn't mean they're appreciative of you. Furthermore, my rules are not meant for every person I go on a date with, and sometimes giving the benefit of the doubt can result in me being disrespected. If you have rules, understand they are interchangeable when you try to date someone new, especially if he's talking to you crazy with a beard that doesn't connect and an outfit that looks like he's selling life insurance.

Red Flags
Super defensive from first meeting.
Spoke very negatively about women and relationships.
Excessive lip licking. Think LL Cool J in the desert.

Green Flags
Great Pad Thai.

Dating Lesson: If he's waiting for the "right" girl, it's not you.

I've always been the right girl, contrary to what the men I've dated think.

I've met quite a few men who have suffered from right girl syndrome. It's found predominantly in non-committal men. The right girl symptoms include comments like, "I'm willing to get married for the right girl," or "I want to slow down for the right girl," and my personal favorite, "I'm just waiting for the right girl."

Rampant in the online dating community, all the men I dated who suffered from the right girl syndrome were all emotionally unavailable. I'd normally hear about her during conversations about relationships and an excuse as to why, at 40, their longest relationship was with a mobile carrier. The way she was brought up in multiple conversations felt like she cooked Michelin-rated meals, folded and put away laundry one-handed, and her vagina smelled like freshly baked cookies after the gym. The type of uniqueness and influence she must've had to change a man's moral compass or hard-to-shake ideals while my dog barely listened after eight years of training. Whoever she was, my curly hair, gorilla grip coochie, and ability to drive at night were no competition. Yet I was interested in who this woman was and how I could become her.

Repeatedly, I'd hear about her from the same type of men with the same excuses around commitment. They were only willing to change for the specific faceless woman, and, seemingly, I never fit the mold. In an attempt to show whoever it was that maybe I was her, I'd change myself for the chance of a spark or chemistry. Without success, we'd break up and my hate for her turned inward. I'd sabotage potential relationships with bitterness that made me compare myself to other girls that she could be. Exhausted from the emotional roller coaster of trying to be someone else but myself, I realized the anomaly of the right girl was nothing more than an excuse for why he'd never be able to commit to me.

The hard truth is most of the men I dated who suffered from the right girl syndrome knew who she was, or at least knew it wasn't going to be me. Whether the one who got away, or an idea of someone who might show up in their future, the right girl was a specific person. If it weren't, he wouldn't have told me that. Instead of comparing myself to an ideal of "her," the idea of conforming to be the right girl with the wrong man started to haunt my dreams.

Every time a relationship ended with a man who suffered from the right girl syndrome, it felt like I dodged a bullet. I stopped trying to be her and instead looked at her as a red flag. She was the "I'm not ready for a relationship" or "I thought we were just friends" get-out-of-jail-free card, an excuse for the lack of consideration.

We wrack our brains and compare ourselves to the idea that the right girl is better than us, or so unique that he'll change, but it only makes us conform to inauthentic things in the process. If she's the one that got away, it was for a reason. If she's a figment of his imagination, there's a reason why she's not here. It simply boils down to his convenience and self-fulfillment. If a man tells you he's waiting for the right girl, it's his dusty mother since she's been the only person that can deal with his non-committal ass.

Dating Lesson: Not all beautifully wrapped packages should be opened.

The Fine Hangry Baby (FHB).

I'm not myself when I'm hungry. I'll admit a lot of my dating mishaps have happened over food, whether it be dinner, my low blood sugar, or someone eating off my plate without asking. For first dates, the free meal is sometimes the hardest part.

I met the FHB organically at work. He was younger, very handsome, and had the best teeth. While these were the best things about him, it was also the worst because he had the cockiness of a handsome man in his mid-twenties with the best teeth. We met when he needed something from my department, and I was the person to help. After that, he came to my department pretty regularly with flirtatious comments. Over the span of a couple of weeks, our chats turned into exchanging numbers with a plan to meet soon.

Before he made plans for a date, I knew the FHB was never going to be anything more than something nice to look at. He was cocky, a little goofy (but not in a good way), and our mentalities were worlds apart. I'd be open to being friends with benefits, but that was the extent of wherever this was going.

He planned a date at a museum and what he said was a nice dinner after. The museum was great until he learned that you're not supposed to touch the art, and you have to read to understand what the exhibit is actually about. I felt like I was an au pair to a bratty kid between the amount of bathroom breaks or comments about being hungry. After about an hour of asking when I was ready to leave, I made the adult observation that someone was getting hangry, and we left. I was surprised he picked such a cool exhibit, so I was looking forward to the free meal as my payment for babysitting.

Once we left the museum, I let him take the lead. Walking to the car, he asked, "Have you ever had Bonchon Chicken?" Unsure of why he asked, I thought to myself, "You mean the Korean double fried chicken fast food restaurant that makes me regret every life decision almost immediately after I eat? Yes, me and my bathroom are very familiar!" Instead of saying what I really wanted to say, I simply replied, "Yes." To which he said, "I don't believe you." For reference, Bonchon Chicken is like asking someone if they've heard of Panera Bread where I'm from. To my luck, his disbelief resulted in us sitting across from each other waiting for our server...with Bonchon menus.

Before the server came, he was lying on his side of the booth, complaining about being hungry. I debated getting an order of fries for the table and a kid's menu for him to color on. This wasn't my first rodeo; I'd babysat in high school. The server even noticed, looking at me to translate his tantrum to adult. "He wants the soy-garlic eight-count and a side of French fries."

While we waited for our food, he transitioned from the booth to lying over the table waiting. Our conversations never went past how hungry he was and how he couldn't wait to eat. I watched the televised game playing at the bar. The food came and, after a couple of bites, his hanger subsided. He was ready to focus his attention on me. "I want you, and I'm not going to stop until I get it," he said. I suppose the fried fat went directly to his brain. I rolled my eyes without a response. Any chance of us having sex left before he ever mentioned chicken. We finished up our meal and he moved next to me on my side of the booth with a failed kiss attempt. After he drove me to my car, I said I'd see him in the office.

The days following our date were normal. I am not a proponent of dating coworkers, but since he was in a different department, I knew I didn't have to see him often. I did get the "I want to see you" text to which I responded with, "Respectfully, no thank you." I blocked him from texting me but then got a message on WhatsApp saying similar sentiments. I blocked him there, too.

The dangers that come with dating some of the best-looking, cockiest men are that they know it and show their ass rather quickly. The next time you're on a first date with a potential man-child, be sure to have an iPad or your phone fully charged, anticipating the "Do you have games on your phone?" question.

Red Flags
iPad Kid.
Aggressive.
Whiney.

Green Flags
Fine as hell.
Smelled amazing.
Nice body.
Teeth like Mr. Clean.

Dating Lesson: Where there's smoke, there's a non-committal man.

Puff Puff Purpose.

I look at the success of things in numbers. When applying for jobs, looking for an agent, or even the amount of money I saved at the grocery store, the numbers never lie. But also, the numbers remind you of the 600 jobs you applied to and didn't get, the no response from those 50 pitch emails, and the fact that you actually spent twice as much to get the sale. For dating in numbers, my method was multiple dates a week with speed rounds of interview-type questions about intentionally dating and what they wanted for the future.

There's no time for small talk when you're dropping eggs monthly and have a Pinterest board full of engagement ring ideas. Over time, the pattern of meeting the men who said they were dating intentionally would end due to a lack of commitment. I couldn't understand where the disconnect came from, but then I got an answer.

I met the Hookah Man unexpectedly one night at a salsa club in the city. He kept trying to dance with me, and after having a couple of drinks to forget my lack of rhythm, we ended up bachata-ing to Aventura until 3am. He was handsome, bulky, and short. I remember feeling his little hands on my hips as he yelled in my ear about his hobbies while Daddy Yankee played. He mentioned multiple times about liking hookah, and, while odd, after a couple of beers no response mattered. We exchanged numbers with the promise of a date next week. Unsuspectingly, Hookah Man remembered. I was surprised to get a time and location to meet a couple of days later.

This was my first time actually meeting someone organically, and my nerves were all over the place. I hoped he looked and acted like what I remembered from my beer goggles. He seemed to live really far away, so the midpoint was an hour away from my home, and I was late. He was extremely patient and, when I got there, he was very excited. We sat down. He'd already started eating and handed me a plate. He smiled a lot, and the conversation was consistent with our first interaction. After ordering my drink and our entrees, I started my first round of heavy-hitting questions. His responses were rather generic: looking for a partner, he wanted marriage and children at some point. As the conversation continued, I started to notice some quirks.

For one, his endless dead fish stare at my boobs. I was wearing a black racerback without a bra, and he clearly noticed. It was so blatant that, at one point, I stopped talking and watched him watch me in a nipple stare-off. Unfortunately, that wasn't the worst of it; he brought up hookah, again. "I have many pipes. Six with two more on the way!" he said. I did that awkward laugh when you don't know what else to do and got a to-go box. Still, I wasn't immediately turned off. Hookah's cool, right? He paid for the check and made it a point to walk me to my car in a well-lit parking lot before 10pm.

He started to do that thing where he was only looking at my lips to go in for the kiss. I could feel it coming. After a couple of sentences of what sounded like mumbling since

I was anticipating when it was going to happen, he put his hand on the back of my back and tongue-kissed me. We were making out on a first date in a chain restaurant parking lot. I peeked to see him, and the dead fish stare lived on. His eyes were wide open the entire time. It was one of the oddest interactions I had with someone. He opened my car door and I escaped. Once I got home, he texted me how great of a time he had.

The rest of the week, we talked through text and some FaceTime calls with plans of getting together sometime in the coming weeks. In the time between us seeing one another again, I started to notice his "hobby" was starting to become the focus of every conversation. On the phone, I could hear the water bubbling from every pull between sentences and, when texting, I'd get a picture of him with a pipe in his mouth before leaving for work. At one point, my "wyd" text received a picture response of him at a hookah lounge at 11am. Who knew they opened that early? For all the times he talked about hookah, we did talk about other things, like him moving to a new apartment and what he wanted in a relationship.

One night in particular, we had an in-depth conversation about his perception of intentionally dating and it shifted my assumptions. My idea of intentionally dating means questioning if this person could be someone I want to have a future with: marriage and kids for the long term. Little things like excessive drinking, credit scores, income, lifestyle choices, and family are all considered in intentionally dating. If it all checks out, we would be in a partnership.

For him, it was quite the opposite. For him, intentionally dating was considering a relationship day by day. No partnership, no family visits, or play dates. Nothing. The universal understanding is that everyone's looking for the same thing, and Hookah Man was the example that there can be multiple interpretations based on individual expectations. He also suffered from "right girl" syndrome.

He made plans for us to have a surprise day of festivities, with the location to be determined. I thought dinner and maybe a day excursion, but I learned very quickly that was not happening. "I'm going to bring my pipe, and we can hang at your place," he said as he held his breath from another pull. Offended that his presumption was he could come to my house and smoke; I knew this was my way out. I expressed my boundary of having strangers at my house, and he apologized multiple times. In an attempt to redirect the conversation, he blurted, "I have a place we can go to!" I am not joking, he recommended a hookah bar.

Immediately, I dropped the bomb that I had asthma, and while smoking was his prerogative, I had to pass on the blueberry mint tobacco and growing stash of illegal pipes. He said one was from Russia. I wasn't one to come between a person and their addiction (I mean passion), but I would never ask a person I'm dating to change the things they enjoy. I didn't want the responsibility of breaking that habit for him.

With no hard feelings, the Hookah Man taught me a great lesson about intention and how it can have a completely different meaning depending on the person. Once I understood this, it was easier to assess how it would fit into my personal timeline of dating. For example, I want to be married after a year of dating, and the person I'm dating might not consider marriage until after a minimum of three years. Instead of asking the "What are your intentions" questions, I started to pay attention to personality traits and lifestyle choices instead of taking surface-level conversations as fact.

Side note: the new apartment he mentioned earlier was "too small to house all his pipes."

Red Flags
Hookah coals.
Hookah hose.
Hookah pipe.
Blueberry Mint flavored tobacco.
Hookah lounges.

Green Flags
Sweet.
Kind.
Employed.

Stop believing the same person who won't commit to a yearly gym membership is going to give you a relationship because he's intentionally dating. Instead, take the person right in front of you as is and judge their consistency and actions towards you. People seek companionship for different reasons, whether arm candy or emotional fulfillment.

Dating Lesson: Beware of the charm of Mr. Right Now.

Take the pressure off finding love by spending time with someone who doesn't require it.

I'm unsure if I've ever met Mr. Right, but I've met many Mr. Right Now's. My first one needed Starbucks Wi-Fi to call me for our first date. We met at a busy coffee shop in the East Village and once the bill came, we split the two coffees and pastries. I assume it was $14 max. He was quirky, non-committal, and unapologetically himself. We spent the night talking about everything you don't expect on a first date, and while he kept trying to touch my ass, it was an entertaining, carefree evening. Inevitably, we went on a couple more dates and that was the end of it. No drama, no long text messages.

In short, "Mr. Right Now" is the person who comes sporadically throughout your dating journey as a reminder of your growth. He's normally hilarious, easygoing, and low-maintenance. While some are harder lessons than others, dating for a temporary fix of attention and excitement showed me my new limitations and offered me acceptance of what I wasn't willing to deal with as I evolved.

My second experience with another Mr. Right Now was not as easygoing as the first. His resume was quite impressive. With a career in banking and a strong family background, he was very mature. While not necessarily my type, I was attracted to his intelligence and demeanor. He made plans for us to meet during the week at a nicer restaurant closer to me out of courtesy.

For once, I arrived on time and he was late. My anxiety was high hoping he wouldn't notice my poker face if he wasn't what I expected. Once he showed up, I felt like I was on the World Poker Tour. He was, dare I say it, really tiny. Yes, in the age of body positivity we accept all body forms, but if I can pick you up, I'm not letting you put it down. I said what I said. His profile only had close-up photos, which normally is fine since I'm 5'2 (well, 5'1 ½), but now we're standing side by side, eye level waiting for our reservation. I remember watching his little legs as we walked to our table.

Once we sat down, the conversation was consistent but generic. We compared war stories of bad relationships well into our entrees. I could tell he was modest based on his responses to my questions and his facial reactions to my "fuck it" mentality. He said wanted to be married again. Considering how he crossed his legs like this was a business meeting, I believed him. We finished the evening with me having dessert since he "wasn't a dessert person" and parted ways soon after. We decided to meet again for lunch in the city.

It was hot, and this time, I was late. He picked a cute tapas restaurant for brunch with charcuterie boards and pickled vegetables. Unsure of how I was going to feel since the first date had no qualms but lacked the zest to get me excited, I was open to seeing him again. When I arrived, he'd already ordered a few small plates in anticipation. He greeted me with a little more enthusiasm than the first time, which was nice. I remembered his little legs as he sat in his corporate stance. The conversation flowed until he said something that immediately ended the date.

"My kids won't be around gay people." He said it like he was an anonymous bot in someone's Instagram comments. I was taken aback by how he said it with such confidence. Intrigued, I had to ask for clarification, to which he responded, "If and when I have children, I will not be comfortable having them around gay people." I wanted to immediately grab a to-go box (because I'm leaving with something), but instead, I just responded with, "I have many people I love that are gay, and this is simply something I will not tolerate." He said he admired my response instead of throwing my water and storming out. Needless to say, we quickly got the check.

As we walked out, I told him the waiter hit on me when he was in the bathroom. He asked why I didn't tell him earlier and my response was, "I wasn't going to tell you until I found out you were a bigot," and sarcastically laughed. Walking to my car, he offered me a ride, his final attempt to salvage what was left. "I don't take rides from homophobes!" I said as I walked to my car.

The irony was he looked just like one of my gay best friends, but with less style and personality. I love you B!

When I first started dating, I was willing to bend and change for the opportunity to have someone. I had sex when I wasn't ready, did the things I didn't enjoy, and agreed to choices I knew weren't sustainable. As time went on, those relationships fizzled, as expected, and I was left with the shame that I gave all of myself to yet another person who didn't deserve it. Instead of allowing myself to further feel the residual indignity, I practiced dating Mr. Right Now.

Whether it's the cheapest person you'll ever meet or the bigot in disguise, you learn a lot from dating Mr. Right Now. Their benefits alleviate the fear of finding the one, but also are exemplary of the unexpected things that happen on the quest for love. In the meantime, savor the dinners, sip and paints, and concerts before learning he can navigate the happy hour menu at Applebee's better than his own life.

Dating Lesson: It's like riding a bike with no wheels and a backward helmet.

Ow, you're on my hair!

Having sex for the first time after my divorce was an out-of-body experience. I was so nervous that I covered my face from the embarrassment. I'd been used to the same person seeing me naked for years. I was unaware of what the kids were doing nowadays. Despite my worry that he'd notice my left breast being bigger than my right, that I hadn't shaved my legs in two months, or why I was wearing period panties on a non-period day, it happened.

Admittedly, I hadn't experienced a real orgasm when I was married. No shade to that man, I think it was in part of me barely knowing my own body or even what to do down there. I never explored my body, which resulted in my inability to express what I needed. I'd hear my girlfriends brag about wild nights and wonder what that was like. I couldn't relate. I never wanted to have sex with my then-husband. My libido would be libi-no for the rest of my life. Until it wasn't.

Once we finished, we laid in bed, and I was uncertain how to feel. We were in a relationship, and he'd been very sweet, but the newness of sex after so long was a bit awkward. I think I would've handled it better with someone who immediately left afterward, but this was someone who I had feelings for, and this consummation had meaning, intimacy, and cuddling. I sat there for a couple of moments before bolting to the bathroom to pee and collect my thoughts.

I sat on the toilet, and the realization that I just had sex hit me as I peed. I smiled. It was pretty good. I wiped and went to the sink to wash my hands. Looking at myself in the mirror, the weight of my anxiety released, I felt lighter. This wasn't infatuation or relief of it being over. I felt confident about my body.

My sex life had always been focused on the man. It was about what he liked and how much he enjoyed it. I'd cramp from positions that'd "hit the spot." It'd start to hurt, and I'd put on my best porn star moaning in hopes it'd expedite the process. It was a one-person job, which made it feel like a duty. Up to this point, I'd never experienced a man doting over my body.

I'd never heard how soft my skin was or had someone play with my hair. Someone taking their time to figure out what worked and who made our experience mutually important was something I had never experienced. I felt empowered. There wasn't guilt when my knees couldn't stay in a certain position long enough, or holding on a little longer because he was almost there. It was just questions about my comfort and admiration of how sexy I was. This new feeling was a glimpse into my future of sexual liberation.

Sex now is on my terms. I do it when I want and make myself the priority. There's no more faking it or moaning to make sure he's satisfied. If it's not good, there's a conversation based on how much I care or an understanding of what I need. Sex is supposed to be fun and intimate for everyone involved, and if not, I'm no longer accepting it. I refuse to talk myself into sexual chemistry again. I used to be the Eminem in 8 Mile before having sex. "Palms are sweaty, knees weak, arms are heavy." There was a disconnect between my mind, body, soul, and vagina. Once I saw I was in control and the privilege that came with experiencing my body, I felt determined that anyone lucky enough to get a taste needed to come correct.

You are a sexual fucking goddess, and if you're not enjoying every bit of your sex life, get a new one. It doesn't have to be on the chore list after washing dishes or doing laundry. It can be a morning delight or dessert before dinner. Don't accept a life of emotionless missionary and aggressive doggy. Advocate for yourself when you're not enjoying the process. Embrace your sensual side and remember the power you hold by expressing what you need. Life is too short not to be having sex with people that want to devour you.

Dating Lesson: Dating the bad boy has residual damage.

*"I knew he was bad for me,
so why did I wait till he'd taken everything?"*

Hollywood's made millions off the leather jacket-wearing, smoking-cigarette, toxic man that sways the innocent high school cheerleader with his nontraditional views. The highest of highs and the lowest of lows, it's all fun and games until you're running to a friend's house at 3 o'clock in the morning after a fight. It's only until you've had a bad boy in real life that you understand just how detrimental he actually is.

My first bad boy had all the quintessential things: an accent, what seemed like a lot of disposable income, and he hated his mother. He was different than any man I'd ever met at that point, very masculine and deliberate with me, but also spontaneous and fun. I remember our first date ended with us dancing at an impromptu basement bar in Soho at 4am. There was something I felt physically about him that night that told me this would end in catastrophe, but the bad boy effect was so consistent it felt like I had no choice except to be with him.

The bad boy effect was his determination to have me. Calls, texts, gifts, planning dates, saying everything I wanted to hear, gaslighting, and love bombing, he left me no time to answer the question of whether I even liked him. I kept feeling like this was the wrong decision, but I could also hear my internal monologue saying, "Don't block your blessings," and, "He's doing everything you want." Similarly to drugs, it felt like a high from all the things he was doing. The more he gave, the more I talked myself into staying.

Then, after a couple of months, came the repercussions of staying.

I planned a surprise birthday party with some of his work friends I found on Instagram. The plan was to go to dinner and then a surprise meet-up at a bar called The Late Late in Manhattan. Since it was a surprise, I texted his friends with the timing of his arrival. After dinner, we headed to the bar. Once we got there, he was excited to see his friends and it looked like the making of a good night until he got drunk. About an hour into the night, his demeanor started to slowly change. He was less jolly and happy and more annoyed and bothered. This was our first night out together with a group, so I never took the change in attitude as anything more than being a bad drunk. Then he turned it on me.

"You want to sleep with my friend Oscar? You're a slut!" He yelled, making a scene in the packed bar. "You're a fucking slut!" He was enraged, and I was confused as to who Oscar was and what exactly he was talking about. Unsure of how to proceed, I did what I assumed was the best route and tried to get him to calm down.

"What are you talking about?" I responded. I remember his grimace as I waited for a response.

"Fuck you!" He yelled. After a couple of tries to come to an understanding, I decided to call an Uber and leave. People around us tried to calm him down, to which he threw water in the face of one of his female coworkers and the whole place went wild.

I waited outside, wearing the tiniest bit of clothing, for my $40 Uber. The traffic was bad, so I had to wait for it to reassign a new driver. After about ten minutes, he came out even more angry, on a tirade to inform all of Manhattan I was a slut. People were staring, and I let him berate me with lies. Following him was Oscar, trying to reiterate he didn't know who I was. That's when he tried to fight Oscar in the street. This person was like nothing I had experienced. He had relentless rage that was uncontainable. I caught a ride with some of his friends who saw me waiting and went home. Once I got in, I vowed to never be with this person and break it off for good. Then the bad boy effect happened again.

He came to my house a wreck, full of excuses and apologies. I let him sleep it off, and we'd talk in the morning. He woke up hungover, and like the person I met before. He kept apologizing and saying he was embarrassed about what he remembered of the night. For the next year, my life was a turbulent emotional thrill ride of apologies, high highs, and extremely low lows. I lost weight, stopped telling friends about my problems, and put myself in some scary situations.

I'd make excuses for his behavior to my detriment. I'd tell myself, "Things will get better," or "We had a really good couple of weeks," disregarding the damaged door from a temper tantrum or my favorite t-shirt ruined from a night when he came home drunk. I'd account for the gifts he bought after he destroyed everything in his path and the sex being amazing. It was the only time we weren't fighting.

The once charming and "rough around the edges" persona was emotionally inept, had a drinking problem, and instigated fights for the hell of it. He was toxic, impatient, and had outbursts that left me mentally and emotionally depleted. His words would be spiteful, and his apologies were empty. I left after an argument that ended in a broken bowl with hot oatmeal splattered all over my living room wall. After repeatedly saying I was done, I mustered up the courage to leave. The residual effects of dating the bad boy were all I needed to know when it came to listening to myself.

From the unnecessary stress to the lying to friends and family that I was okay when I wasn't, choosing the bad boy cost me my dignity, sanity, and health. Also, let me say no advice given to me was something I hadn't considered. It's easy to tell people to leave without seeing the fear of being unable to or what it means if I had to come back. As the red flags continued to line up, I repeatedly had the conversation that it'd get better or make the excuse that he was stressed and didn't mean it. I knew after the second drunken tirade this relationship was not sustainable, but I prioritized his well-being over my own instead of simply saying "no" from the beginning.

Alternate Ways of Saying "No"
"Absolutely not."
"No, thank you."
"You are cute, but not that cute."
"This is not working out for me."
"I hope you understand, but hell no."
"Oh, you got me fucked up."

"FUCKKKKKKKKKKKKKKKKKKKKKKKKKKKK No."
"I'm no longer interested."
"Sir, respectfully, go to hell!"
"Get the fuck out of my house!" [for more aggressive cases]

Best ways to know when to say "No"
When your friends hate him.
When he makes jokes at your own expense.
When your mom doesn't ask how he's doing after she met him.
When he uses alcohol as an excuse for his behavior.
When they don't wait for you to get into the house.
When your Abuelita, who barely speaks English, calls him the devil.
When his mother doesn't talk to him.
When you physically can feel his bad energy: nervous and bitter.
If he ever throws anything, even a party, unless it's on your behalf.
If he has temper tantrums. Even one.

Dating the bad boy has a lot of highs and lows. When you have a physical, mental, or emotional question of, "is this relationship is meant for you?" leave and say no. The bad boy effect is meant to break you down and drain you until you're making excuses for an abuser. That person was never meant to be in your life. Let him be the lesson that your boundaries are a protection of self. Use them.

Honorable mentions.

To the one ex-boyfriend who keeps spamming me with promotional emails to reset a 7/11 account password and coupons to Long Horn Steakhouse: Would it hurt you to sign me up for places I at least enjoy, like Red Lobster?

"Expand your palate."

To the man who matched with me and ghosted me after a couple of text messages, only for me to circle the block and have him remind me he ghosted: You're right, our personalities wouldn't match. For starters, you don't have one (zing) and for finishers, I'm pretty sure I saw you at a local seafood boil restaurant recently, and I hated your shirt!

"Well, that was rude."

To the man who took me on a joy ride in his Hell Cat without telling me he'd been drinking, only to race random people on the highway at speeds of 100 mph: I read your email and I appreciate you telling me I was right about what I said. Duh.

"You owe your neighbors an apology!"

To the man I matched and immediately unmatched after we FaceTimed: You didn't tell me about that one aggressive tooth you had.

"Normally, it's you, but this time, it was certainly me."

To the man who made dinner plans within minutes of matching, only to tell me how I should be doing things in my own home, how he has rules for dogs and ways of order I'd have to adhere to.

"Cesar Milan would approve this date cancellation."

To the man who returned from the dating underworld on Valentine's Day after not responding for over eight months with a, "Hey, what happened to you?"

"Sir, I've been on the couch, unbothered."

To the man who left me at the pizza shop to chase carjackers who broke into his car and had his grandmother pull up during her shift at Big Bus with the double-decker to see what was going on (she parked in the middle of the street while we talked to the police about the entire altercation): I'm happy you didn't die or get meat lover's pizza. I hate sausage on pizza, especially leftovers.

"Can I get a box for this?"

A personal list of "Icks."

I donated my vagina to science, I mean dating, and ended up with a longer list of "icks. The art of ick detection can only be explained as a feeling. Below are many I've encountered throughout my life.

- The face of the slow lean in for a first kiss.
- The noise his flip-flops make when they're wet.
- Having a food or gluten allergy.
- Closing an umbrella.
- The one vein in the middle of his forehead when he tries to lift something heavy.
- Him waiting for a fist bump to be reciprocated.
- Looking at his feet and squatted legs during sex.
- Watching him look for you at the beach after the tide pulled him away.
- The thought of him pooping naked.
- Him repeating a comment when no one heard the first time.
- The idea of him choking in public.
- The spit or grease balls that get stuck in the corner of his mouth.
- Not being able to get a noticeable booger after two attempts.
- When he shakes while picking me up during sex.
- Watching him crawl over the driver seat since you parked too close to the other car.
- Seeing the patchy hair on his upper thigh.

- The way his body coils when you tickle him.
- Wearing loafers without socks.
- Thinking of him waiting for the water to get hot before a shower.
- Watching him strain to get something he can't reach.
- Not being able to merge in stand-still traffic.
- Trying to balance his plate on his lap at a picnic.
- If he sits crisscross on a swivel chair.
- If he's in someone's way and doesn't hear someone say "excuse me" the first time and they have to say it louder.
- If he says "I'm cold" or "it's raining" in a baby \ voice.
- When he tells people he listens to The Joe Rogan Experience.
- If he kisses family members on the mouth.
- Watching him try to find his straw and missing when he goes to take a drink.
- Fulltime mouth breathers outside of sleeping.
- If he's afraid of dogs.
- If he says things like "me like-y" or "me want-y."
- Wearing those super tight skinny jeans with the rips and ripples.
- If he stands up immediately after the plane gets to the loading gate and you're three rows from the last.
- If he uses his whole tongue to lick the salt off of a margarita.
- The grunt he makes when he holds his breath trying to put his socks on one-handed.

To whom it may concern.

Over and out.

I'm writing to inform you I've decided to sign off immediately and never return ever again. When I first started, I was enthusiastic about the opportunity to meet and eat with some of the hottest bachelors within a 30-mile radius, but my attempts at finding love have left me with a residual bitterness and hate towards dating culture and the male species entirely.

I can't say I've enjoyed my time wasted on your apps, but I appreciate the opportunities for personal development that have been provided during my tenure. However, after much consideration for my mental health, I've decided to pursue really anything that doesn't include telling a stranger how my day's going.

I want to express my deepest gratitude for the opportunity to pay money to see more likes, have more roses, and have a chance at love through currency, but I've learned you're only around to keep me engaging, not to actually get engaged. Moving forward, I am committed to fulfilling my love life by unlearning some of the habits that can be difficult when pursuing a new relationship, but it will be without your assistance. So it is with a heavy heart that I give my resignation effective immediately.

Respectfully,
Never again.

"Dating me is like a roller coaster: Nervous before getting on, enjoying the ride, and immediately regretting those two hotdogs after." - Nikki Frias, Hinge Profile 2022

Always gonna give you up
Always gonna let you down
Always gonna run around and desert you
Always gonna make you cry
Always gonna say goodbye
Always gonna tell a lie and hurt you.

…If Rick Astley* was a fuckboy.

*Hector Hint: Rick Astley released the song "Never Gonna Give You Up (Pianoforte) in 1987.

Chapter Four:

GIVING UP.

The realities learned from throwing back
all the fish in the sea.

Giving Up: Being Single AF means Single and Flourishing.

I'm letting the universe handle the love department for once.

I've never been intentionally single. I'd vow to never return after every lost connection, but it wouldn't be uncommon to answer a text or two from an unsaved number. So, for the first time ever, I'm sticking to my word by being Single AF and remembering what's important beyond matching pajamas and figuring out love languages.

There are no upcoming dates, no DMs, no surprise "Hey, long time no talk" messages. Everyone's blocked and everything's deleted. I refuse to give up on finding love, I'm just no longer unmatching and going on second-chance dates. Instead of rationalizing the lack of chemistry, different values, and lifestyle of a potential new partner— I'm doing something that doesn't come naturally: I'm no longer forcing anything.

I'm over the positivity of getting back on the horse after another disappointment and reaffirming statements that he's still out there. Maybe he isn't, or at least, not online. I've taken so much advice and comments that, at this point, I am no longer accepting suggestions in my box (literally). I don't want to hear another thing about boys, talk about my dating life, or hear how "it'll happen when you least expect it." Instead, I'm taking a year to unlearn what I thought about dating and appreciate the things about myself that aren't so closely tied to having a title or a commitment.

I saw something the other day that said, "Your relationship is the least interesting thing about you." I hope to one day have the clarity of living that same sentiment. Uncertain when it will happen and with who, there's no doubt that love will find its way to me again. I just need to not be so dependent on a specific type for my own fulfillment.

She said, "Come and find me!"
as she sat on the couch, unbothered.

The only guarantee to happiness
is stimulus checks.

Life be life-ing.

One day on my trip to the gym, my car started making the noises people make in car commercials. After my workout, I decided to stop at AutoZone, assuming everyone was a mechanic, and someone knew exactly what to do. I walked in like the damsel in distress I decided to be and said, "My car is making a noise. Can you fix it?" Unenthused, the teenager said, "No," and I left the store without a resolution.

Like any minor inconvenience, I called my best friend to vent and complain, hoping it'd make me feel better. Angrily, I waited for her to pick up the phone, and before she could get out a "What happened?" I said, "If I had a man, this would've never happened. I wouldn't be doing this by myself!" No room for, "This is going to cost me a fortune, or I might have to take a day off from work," I decided in that moment to make my lack of a relationship the reason for my Hyundai hindrance. Waiting for my unwavering supportive response of, "Girl, yes. Fuck them all." My best friend said, "When you had a man, you still had to do it," and in true best friend fashion, she dropped the mic. I wasn't expecting it, but she was completely right. I've always equated having a relationship with my life being easier and more fulfilling.

We could probably find my logic on relationships tucked in a book between learning how to be a homemaker from the 1970s, and the influence of misogyny. But, in short, I've put my validation into having a partner because it's a narrative that's been reiterated throughout my life.

It started in grade school, singing on the swings, "First comes love, then comes marriage," up until hearing "Wish for a man!" as I blew out my 34th birthday candles. Even the women I've heard about throughout history have always had a man; Eve had Adam, Bonnie had Clyde, and Jackie had John. I, too, have noticed most conversations tend to end in boys since giving up dating. Now more noticeable, the shift from talking to and about boys to having nothing has allowed me to relearn the role romantic relationships play in my own life and why I'm so obsessed with having one.

A glutton for punishment, it all resulted in the idea of how much better I'd be with a partner, which then evolved to my Hyundai hindrance and a constant comparison of myself and others. For example:

[Hearing a slow song at a concert]
"It would be amazing if I had someone to share this moment with."

[Seeing people coexist]
"Why not me?"

[Being sick]
"I wish someone was here to take care of me."

[Binge-watching a new show]
"If only someone could rub my feet."

[Seeing a couple grocery shopping]
"Why can't someone tell me to go get the eggs?"

I compared everyone that was presumably a couple, whether related, friends, or not. I had a problem with them being happy together while I was alone. It became an obsession, and my view became negative. I loathed seeing couples celebrate dinner anniversaries, mocked public displays of affection, and rejected any form of love if it didn't involve me. I knew it was selfish, but I was bitter. I'd been waiting for my opportunity to have things easier and happier, but instead, I was stuck sitting in front of an Auto Zone waiting for a tow truck at 7 o'clock at night.

I kept hearing, "When you had a man, you still had to do it," repeatedly. It's like one of those things you know, but it clicks once you hear it out loud. In my relationships, I did do a lot by myself. Oddly, my expectations for my future relationships were never my reality in relationships prior. Everything was hard and, in some cases, brutal.

I realized my assumptions were nothing more than a fantasy that things would get easier in general. I could depend on someone else to bring the groceries inside or walk the dog without considering the amount of work that came along with adding a new person to my life. But also, there were the risks associated with dating the wrong person. Some nights, I'd cry to myself out of misery as he slept next to me. And even then, I had to do everything on my own.

Life happens to everyone, even with a man. To assume a relationship can automatically alleviate the perils of life is unrealistic. For some, it can mean more stress, work, and disappointment once you actually get into one. Instead of having a love-hate relationship with everyone else around you, remind yourself why you're single. It's not because you can't find a person. It's because all the

people you've met till now aren't worth the resources needed to try and make it sustainable. Some relationships can be great, but never assume it's a savior to all your daily struggles. He still has to go to work.

You don't need a partner at this moment,
you need an oil change.

Well, it *looked* easy.

This chapter is dedicated to Jenn Lucero.

Being from Virginia, routine local winery trips are pretty common in the summer. While trying to forget my decision to wear jeans in what feels like 120 degrees, I'd sip my $12 glass of Pinot Noir from 2022 and entertain my married friends with stories that led to my nonexistent dating life. Reminding them of the streets they left oh so long ago, I'd conclude with, "I just want things to be easy," and take another sip out of frustration. As we polished off another bottle and finished the gooey parts of the brie rind, my friend Jenn said something that changed my entire perspective on dating.

"Not everyone wants easy, Nik."

I nearly choked on my Costco cracker as I received life-changing advice over my third glass of wine. There are people who will never be okay with easy. Easy as in no emotional manipulation, a mutual understanding of what's inappropriate, both maintaining financial stability, considering feelings and respecting people's property are some examples. Trying to wrap my head around how some thrive off bad situationships*, relationships, and people in general finally made sense. If I'd realized that earlier, I could've protected myself from a lot of previous traumas.

I've dated men who thrived in chaos. They'd make everything a competition, argument, or tantrum. There was never respect for healthy communication and trust. Easy for them was "being his peace*"in the form of me complying and being submissive. We didn't talk about our problems, individual internal battles, or moments of vulnerability. It made me emotionally subservient to a partner that didn't reciprocate. We'd fuck and fight until I couldn't do it anymore, and I'd leave broke, broken, and bitter. I'd wrack my brain trying to understand why easy was so hard. "Easy" was based on my expectations, not someone else's.

In therapy, I talked a lot about the concept of easy. As a high-value woman, it is hard to understand why some of the men I dated created these destructive environments, full of fighting and disrespect, instead of the opposite. I wanted to talk about everyone else being the problem, but in true therapist fashion, the conversation steered to me.

"What is something specific to you that is needed in a relationship outside of morals, etc.?" The question seemed off-topic, but the framed college degrees on the wall had to mean something, so I indulged in the question.

It took me a minute, but I responded, "A good morning text makes me feel validated in relationships." I felt embarrassed saying it out loud since it was trivial, yet also a consistent issue I had when dating. "And some guys don't send them at all."

She asked, "Do you tell them it's what you need?" I responded, "Everyone knows the importance of a good morning text." She paused and then said, "Do they?"

They don't. I've had issues with what I considered consistent communication when it came to texting in my relationships. I assumed all men knew women appreciated a message first thing in the morning. After asking around, I realized it was not as common as I thought. I had some girlfriends who talked to their partner once a day or didn't text at all. So, taking all that into consideration, I couldn't assume everyone thinks like me. For the things I deem easy, like texts throughout the day, what peace looks like, or a clear and honest understanding of decency, it might not be so easy for others.

Therapy helped me figure out what I considered easy in relationships by getting clear on the things I needed (big and small) to maintain the relationship. For big things, fidelity and trust were on the list; for the small things, some were consistent date nights or activities we could do as a couple and good morning/night texts. It's my responsibility to let my partner know what I need, and while it can be disappointing or disheartening when someone finds that to be asking for a lot, it comes with the territory.

In any new relationship, the mutual ease that both people have starts with discussing what is needed and then respecting it through action. We all have different manuals and require additional parts. Ease comes after the relationship is established with that mutual understanding. Until then, know it's subjective and not exclusive. For those we encounter who make "easy" look like toxic behavior and stupid mind games that'll leave you confused, let them marinate in their own trauma.

When understanding what is easy, recognize it's not that easy for everyone.

*Hector's Hint: A situationship is a fake boyfriend or girlfriend that has all the aspects of a romantic or sexual relationship without the commitment or title.

**Hector's Hint: "Be his peace" is a narrative that, in my opinion, seems to suggest that the burden of peace and stability in a relationship should fall on the woman. It gives Mad Men era, the "men are talking," and "do things to make him happy" vibes.

Dry like the desert.

To my parents, skip this chapter.

Being single and not having consistent sex has started to drive me a little crazy. I'm at that awkward stage of wanting sex often, but also on the cusp of a night in with nachos sufficing. Over time, my bush will forget the distraction of being touched by a man, and I can focus on more important things like getting to work on time, world politics, or capitalism. Until then, I'll fantasize about all the Tom's dicks that are hairy, or something like that.

Some distractions that have helped:

Work out:
Get out the rage in the cage. It satisfies the urge to gyrate and you get skinny in the process. You'll be able to get so tired from all the cardio that the last thing you'll think about is laying in the bed doing contortion acts.

Play Pickleball:
Or something mentally stimulating that'll take your mind off that one fine ass disaster of a man you dated months ago. Join a math club or try to teach yourself Mandarin. Who has time to think about bumpin' uglies when you have to remember the formula for calculating pi?

Eat a lot:
Nobody wants to get stuffed when they're stuffed. Am I

right?

Get a Dog:
Nothing is more shameful than getting your back blown out and catching your adopted two-year-old Pitbull watching in disgust from a crack in the door.

And when all else fails...

Masturbate:
Don't be scared of your body, it's the only real thing you own (unless you ask some members of Congress). Get familiar with learning what makes you feel good. Get a toy, use your hand, watch porn, get freaky. No one has to know, and it will make your dry spell less miserable. For the girlies who've never masturbated: research, invest to see what works for you, and most importantly, have patience. It took me a couple of tries to know what worked for me. This isn't the movies or porn. There might be many times when nothing happens, you have to keep at it! The good news is once you learn what works, you have the secret password, and it gets easier the more you do it. Last thing! Don't forget to wash your hands and toys—no, but seriously.

To my parents that I know didn't skip this chapter because y'all nosey. I ask you never bring this up at any family gathering, social setting, or room we ever share together moving forward. Please and thank you.

When you want it too bad.

"Too much intention causes tension."

Being single can be a very insular experience. The effort to meet, connect, and maintain a relationship is so critical in the first couple of months. At the height of my dating, I was so intentional that it ended up being the reason why I had to step away. I wanted it too bad.

I couldn't stop thinking about being in a relationship. I'd bring it up to friends and fantasize about it happening often. I'd get on the apps every moment I had downtime, and I'd talk to anyone who matched. I was so consumed with the lifestyle of dating. I'd go on multiple dates during the week and give many chances to people I wasn't interested in. I thought that, statistically, if I dated multiple people at a time, one would eventually turn into a relationship.

With every new person in the hot seat before entrees hit the table, being intentional drove me to not make the best decisions in partners. If someone told me they were dating intentionally, I'd stay. Despite the lack of emotional fulfillment or any chance of sustainment, my logic was that if we wanted the same things, we'd figure it out. The efforts toward finding, meeting, and maintaining a new connection meant showing up for each person with the same energy. The talking felt like a job. After having the same iterations of the same conversation more than once a night, I looked forward to sitting and saying nothing. For me, that says a lot.

I craved connection and wanted to be in a relationship so bad it didn't matter with whom. Clearly, I didn't learn my lesson the first time. My desperation was to my detriment, and it was becoming exhausting. I had to emotionally rebuild myself after every disappointment and overcome the regret of giving myself and my energy to another mediocre man. Forcing a relationship for the sake of saying I had one took all the fun out of naturally meshing with a person. Dates stopped being fun, and texting back felt like a hassle. I knew I had to step away, hoping that I'd one day find him without looking.

Dating without intention in my 30s looks like hoping for the best but saying fuck it if it doesn't happen. There's no more worry over every interaction, hoping it would lead to a relationship. Instead, my priority is: If my pants fit, dessert.

Being pressed to find a relationship will lead you to the wrong relationship. When we want something so bad, we are willing to take anything. Release yourself from the burden of finding a partner and remember a relationship is only a part of you. It isn't you. Contrary to what the entire world has told us, a man will not complete you, especially with a FICO score of 402.

"You just don't force love, you don't force falling in love, you don't force being in love – you just become."
- Juan Pablo Galavis

It's no Gouda.

My relationship with dairy has always been contemptous.

In the words of my closest friend, I always "take the cheese" when it comes to closure in relationships." Taking the cheese" simply means giving a response when provoked. It wasn't uncommon when I'd get a message from someone from my past that, instead of deleting and moving on, I'd give a response and a reaction for decoration. There's something super gratifying about having the last word or reminding yet another random WhatsApp message they lost a real one. Call me Ratatouille*, this bitch is taking the cheese.

I used those messages as a way to legitimize my feelings about myself. I've always feared I'm not loveable, and when I opened up about it, I had a ruthless abusive ex-boyfriend do a good job of weaponizing my love during every fight. He'd say things like, "I know why your ex-husband cheated," or "No one will ever love you," after a spat over the dishes. From a logical perspective, of course, I've maintained long-term relationships with friends and family, and I've since built romantic feelings with new people. But, the hurt feelings that followed someone getting to know you and not wanting you led to years of questioning love in my life. Never mind if the relationship was good enough for me, I've had to accept there are some people who won't see your value.

My charcuterie board of responses never came with changed behavior or the relationship I originally wanted. The apologies were just acknowledgements and an opportunity for his own emotional fulfillment or other selfish reasons. We weren't getting back together, and the closure wasn't life-changing. After sometimes hours of clarifying why I didn't want to be with this person or him mansplaining his trauma in the limited time we spent together, taking the cheese wasted my time and energy on a person who meant nothing in my stratosphere. I had to accept that taking the cheese was purely for ego.

I struggle to accept the natural flow of people coming in and out of my life. Whether for a reason or a season, taking the cheese was my way of controlling an outcome. It didn't matter what they said, I had to ensure they knew how great I was or how much they were missing out. I'd go as far as meeting up with some just to see the sadness and disheveled appearance following Nikki withdrawals, but it was never the case. They all looked the same with fresh haircuts, new clothes, and their bills still paid. Nothing changed for them except another chance to pull me back in and my disappointment of knowing I stopped nothing. The audacity to presume a life of damnation after scorning me, what am I, Medusa?

It's not your job to remind people how great you are, especially the temporary ones. Instead of giving every mishap in love more time and energy with an explanation, remember that some simply don't deserve it. You can't change how others treat or view you, but you can protect your peace by being unreachable or not responding. Trust that better is coming, and the longer you decide to stay in a space of lackluster attempts to

reconnect and drunken "I miss you" texts, you're only hindering what's trying to find you. If you see another text in the form of Gouda, delete it. An email that smells like Mozzarella, it's spam. Or holes in his story like Swiss, block and delete. Everyone knows he fucked up. You don't have to remind him.

Tips to putting down the cheese:

Block and delete.
Blocking is an act of self-love. It is not for the other person. It is for you. See your habits. Do you like to hurt your own feelings by prying into people's lives on social media? Do you keep pictures and old text messages to go through for your nighttime routine? Block and delete all that shit. That's the past. Those messages mean nothing now and the lifestyle you were living online isn't real. Stop giving in to the temptation to respond and get your feelings hurt.

Tempted? Take a Minute.
When you get a message or call, do a lap and see how you feel after. Most of the time you just need some sun on your face and grass between your toes to see your response depletes your energy and only fulfills someone else's ego.

Control what you can.
I will keep saying this till I'm blue in the face. There is always a risk when getting to know someone new. We can only control what we can control. Everything else doesn't deserve the energy or brain power that comes with it. If you're texting to get the last word or convey an unnecessary point, just remember this person is most likely not going to change.

Understand your "why."

Take a minute to answer why you are responding and what you think your response will change. If he's not coming with free money or an inheritance he doesn't want, let it go.

Play on someone else's phone.

*Hector Hint: *Ratatouille* is a Disney movie about a rat chef pursuing his dreams in Paris. Get it? Also, WhatsApp is primarily used for international calls and texts, but it's also a space for people to reach you that have been blocked.

Shocker! The result of not settling is being temporarily alone.

The reaction to action.

Social media makes me feel like the last single person on earth. I hardly know the people on my social media since it's full of children and spouses I've never met. I'd be lying if I didn't say it bothered me at times. In fact, it bothers me a lot more than it should. Between the baby pictures and engagement photos, I find myself wondering how my life would be if I made different decisions. Would I be as happy as everyone's profile picture?

I'd look at the people around me and legitimize myself in their world. I reminisced all the mom-shaming conversations that I shouldn't be a part of because "I wouldn't understand," and slowly accepted that my engaged friends changed from listening to giving advice. The only way I could make sense of it all was by accepting what came with settling. At my lowest, my pep talks would include the "don't settle" conversation and I'd list everything I accomplished to feel better for not having anyone. I got so wrapped up in defending my existence that I diminished my worth to my work. Hence this book and the other copious amounts of workshops, teaching, and writing things I do daily. It feels like my existence is equated to having a functioning uterus and the ability to maintain a contract.

People decide to settle for many reasons.

"I'd known him for over 10 years. It was about time."
"The market was the lowest it's been, so we bought the house."
"We're not getting any younger!"

Admittedly, I had the same logic when I got married at 24. It wasn't the greatest love of all, but after college it's what you did. We'd been together by that point for six years, and after everyone asked when he would make me an honest woman, we married. As you know, it wasn't successful for many reasons, but if I had allowed room for brevity and space to see all those wrong reasons, I could've saved myself the trauma. I was doing what everyone else wanted for me, I didn't even know what I wanted for me. The pressure of being single at 34 was now amplified, and while settling isn't a bad thing, reminding myself what not settling looks like has helped.

"I wish I could find the one already." Too often I hear people talk about the rush to not be single with the fear of settling in the same sentence. I hear people talk about being single as if a relationship hasn't happened for them instead of recognizing they have the choice to be in one. As if singlehood is bestowed on God's least favorite, let me remind you the result of not settling is…drum roll please… being single. This comes as no surprise, but not settling is a choice and being single is the consequence. Which means moments will be celebrated with one less person there and your holiday cards have a little extra room.

The space and mental capacity of choosing and maintaining a relationship requires effort, continuous understanding, and selflessness. Not to mention that one person who we know who'd do any and everything for you is either someone you only see as a friend, or you don't find attractive. The issue is not finding someone, it's finding your someone.

We often feel the need to explain why we choose to stay single, and while many can't understand, sometimes we can't either. We all crave the love and attention that comes with a healthy relationship, but if you aren't willing to accept the current dating pool, know the time in between is the reward of not settling for what you don't want. It takes a lot of courage to choose yourself, and while some won't understand your choices, it doesn't make your decision to wait inferior.

The consequence of not settling will result in attainment.

I've had the privilege of always
having everything I needed:
a loving family, supportive
friends, and different romantic
relationships trickled in for
decoration. I've spent a lot
of time investing in these
relationships and building a place
of comfort with each facet, yet
the love for myself has always
needed work.

Chapter Five:

FALLING IN LOVE.

Learning from a small window of time.

Falling back in love

...with love.

As the Tracee Ellis Ross* of my friend group, my experience of giving up has also allowed me to be more present and appreciative of things. From spaces to people, walks with Griffin, random "I miss you" texts from friends, sending/receiving funny TikTok's, dinner with family, working out, trying a new Trader Joe's soda water, you name it. The search for love has pushed me to love every other aspect of my life more, and to include myself.

As more friends get into serious relationships, I'm doing a lot more things by myself. The sporadic days at wineries now need to be planned weeks in advance, and daily gossip sessions becoming monthly. My friends are the happiest they've ever been, but I've slowly felt the people I depended on slipping away. I don't want to miss the big moments like engagements, baby announcements, or weddings because of my ill relationship with being the third wheel.

Instead of being triggered by my fear of abandonment, this was the finite time when I didn't have to consider anyone else but myself. I show up when I want, leave when I'm ready, and, most importantly, consider no one but myself in the process. There is no delay in figuring out what I'm doing and how I want it done. I get to sit back and appreciate the time I have with my people and focus on bettering myself wholly.

Self-love has always required effort. I appreciate my body, brains, and confidence, but I find it questionable throughout facets of my life. Between relationships with friends, family, and a spouse, the times I've loved myself the most were met with being told I was doing and asking for too much. It's hard to balance what you think you know about yourself and what you're told, which speaks to my inconsistent understanding of myself. Through inner work, conversations with friends, and therapy, I'm getting better at giving myself permission to take up space and knowing the intimacy I crave and its requirements start with me.

This time of stillness has become a form of therapy. I'm doing a deep dive into love to understand the difference between attention, my fear of abandonment, and the need for consistent validation. I am starting to understand what being single means to me and evaluating what the future looks like when it comes to goals, platonic relationships, etc. I want to be ready before getting everything I want.

The window of time to learn about yourself gets smaller after you are filing joint taxes and claiming dependents.

*Hector Hint: Tracee Ellis Ross is an actress best known for her lead roles in shows like Girlfriends and Black-ish, but also her ability to be unapologetically single and fabulous.

Give love, life.

Someone's always listening.

I've talked about self-love in my previous book, and it's something that requires effort every day. It can be shown through picking better food to eat, taking that workout class, or standing in the sun for a couple of minutes before work. One I've yet to master is how I talk to myself and realizing the energy I create around my reality. With love, I'm normally on the front lines at the "Men Are Trash" rally with a sign and trail mix for everyone without a penis. My love life was the punch line of every joke, and my social media was a barrage of women in the same boat, miserable and unhopeful for the future.

I talked about love like it did something to me personally. I spewed the narrative that all men are cheaters, and all the good ones are already taken. My outward detests for love made me the point person for all the complaints as my friends started sending me memes, GIFs, videos of funny unsuccessful love stories (whether podcast or a rant), and complaints about their shitty relationships. I saw in real time that my negative views were starting to become my reputation.

I didn't want to be the go-to person for cheating spouse gossip or unsuccessful relationships. I wanted everything but that. Instead, I wanted to hear about the surprise dates, validation of feeling safe, couples' vacations, healthy communication, and a relationship without trust issues. Don't get it twisted, I'm going to hate (joking...kind of), but at least there'd be an example of what's possible. If I was ever going to survive this new chapter of letting love find me, I needed to create a reality for it.

The internet has been extremely influential on my outlook of men and dating. I'd spend hours changing my brain chemistry through mindless scrolling of doom-dating content. Between the narratives of "if he wanted to, he would," and "men are instinctually non-monogamous creatures," I listened to anyone with a podcast. I regurgitated what I heard, without a developed thought, and noticed it similarly with my single friends. We repeated recycled concepts from influencers and trends intended to keep us engaged, which shifted us from the mindset of "it hasn't happened" to "it will never happen." I started by changing my mental and social algorithm.

I knew I had the power to curate a bubble of positivity, and while I couldn't eliminate the internet completely, I chose to consume it differently. I eliminated the negative social media talk and stopped sending friends the draining TikTok's, reels, and Facebook posts about how terrible men were and the dating pool having piss in it. I blocked accounts that made me feel like shit, and demanded Mark Zuckerberg only send me dogs being funny, pimple-popping videos, and inspirational quotes. In response, my perspective started to change.

I gave more positive advice to friends and looked for the good in relationships. Also, knowing with some friends that's impossible, I'd limit the amount of negativity I heard about their exes or steer the conversations from singlehood being a curse to more of a time of reflection and self-preservation. It's easier to get excited about the unknown than to fear it, and the impact of changing the media I consumed helped significantly.

My overconsumption of the internet made me feel icky. I laughed a little less, didn't enjoy myself enough, and put so much stress on finding someone based on the internet's expectations. I talked to myself negatively and projected my assumptions onto others, which then created a mindset I didn't agree with in reality.

Create an environment conducive to finding someone by consuming media that promotes the positive aspects of you and everyone around you. You can bring anything into your world with a great mindset and faith in knowing what you want will happen one day. The more you conjure up a false reality of how bad your next partnership will be, the more likely it will be. If love is what you want, then stop being so negative about it.

Girl, you're manifesting a terrible relationship without even knowing it!

Recognizing love.

Love is not linear.

My interpretation of love came from movies like *The Notebook* and *10 Things I Hate About You*. It was unmovable, endless, and as persistent as Heath Ledger sang "Can't Take My Eyes off You" by Frankie Valli on the bleachers as Julia Stiles played soccer. Set as the expectation throughout life, my motivation of finding romantic love has since been rooted in cinema without remembering they were paid actors with a written storyline.

I've fantasized about having a husband more than anything else in life. It's been a constant thought for as long as I can remember. I see him waiting for me at the end of the aisle, out to dinner with friends, holding hands during the birth of our children, and sitting on the porch until we're old and gray. He's crept into all parts of my life, with his presence expected to make things just a little bit sweeter. The antithesis of a life worth living, the goal of finding romantic love has been engrained to be of the utmost importance. Unfortunately, being so focused on finding him, I forgot the other types of love that contribute immensely to my life.

Just a reminder: You are so loved. I will say it over and over again.

I've experienced love before I fell into it. My parents, friends, associates, old teachers, ex-boyfriends, old bosses, etc. all shaped my perspective on the world, opened my mind, and educated me and my well-being. Those relationships have been comprised of disappointments, fights, lots of consideration for one another and special memories. I can remember the smell of my grandma making cream of wheat when I was a baby, the first time I learned to ride a bike, and my 7th grade math teacher staying late on Wednesdays to tutor me in fractions. The range of relationships I've had (varying from acquaintances to best friendships) all had different levels of expectations.

Love shows up differently in every relationship. It's a friend telling you how unflattering that one dress is, someone asking, "Did you eat?" after a long day, a gentle "I told you so" after doing the thing they told you not to do. It could be a friend sending you a Galentine's Day Gift, someone saving you a plate at the busy potluck, or a neighbor getting your package outside the door. The little things that show someone's consideration for you without the expectation of anything in return. It's everywhere.

Some require nothing more than how it makes me feel: grass in between my toes, Griffin (my dog) licking my feet to wake me up in the morning, midday naps, watching a stranger help another stranger, listening to Christmas music in the Summer, someone holding the door, volunteering, laughing from an old memory, home cooked meals, my abuela playing with my hair.

Once you recognize the different types of love, it's easier to realize how limited it is to give fully to everyone. Romantic love is amazing, but it's just one part of the love you experience daily. The love around you through companionship, platonic relationships, and moments with family are just as important, if not more. These

relationships span your whole life and represent an evolution of people continuously choosing you. That is beautiful and irreplaceable. Before determining the most important love is the one you meet in the line at Wawa, remember you've already had it all along.

Love finds you every day without acknowledgment.

He knew he wanted me from our first encounter, but that was before he knew about my uncontrollable IBS and intolerance for microwaved leftovers.

Chapter Six:

TAKEN.

"My man, my man, my man."

Taken: Y'all, it happened.

These next chapters I didn't expect to be writing. After getting through the hardest parts of heartbreak, the curiosity of what was next for me evolved from crying to friends to the acceptance that maybe my person was in another country happily married. I've stepped outside of my comfort zone and I'm confident the lessons I've learned from my previous experiences have molded me to be a little bit better about moving through life.

After the past eight months of not entertaining even the thought of another person, I've accepted that I, too, am flawed in love. I've been toxic, hateful, ungrateful, overreactive, and blocked my own blessings. I've played the game and still got my feelings hurt. I've hurt feelings and I've ghosted. Additionally, I had my own unchecked daddy issues, a false perception of partnership, and the habit of continuously tying my value to something. These flaws have appeared in every relationship, from friends and family to even my failed marriage. I'm still processing how to deal, but striving to be a prize without the surprise of my triggers sabotaging every new connection.

A lot of my poor choices in relationships were based on how I viewed myself. I worried about what felt like a closing window to find a person and the assumptions that came with singleness – that I was problematic, a narcissist, or difficult.

These fears have hardened me to be hyper-independent and naturally defensive, but through acceptance, I know that doesn't mean I'm less deserving. Through inner work, I've liberated myself from the expectations I have in love and my partner.

I always worried that I'd never love anyone as much as my ex-husband, and as I step into the new role as girlfriend (*flips hair*), I see a possibility of loving deeper. I've fallen in love without having to forsake myself in the process. I'm softer, more private, and confident from the abundance of emotional support and security. I feel considered and prioritized without asking. Aside from all the feel-good things that come with a budding relationship, my approach to this new love is also different. I appreciate the time we're together, for however long it will last, and I trust the natural flow of relationships. I knew it would come again, and though uncertain with whom, there was no doubt he'd be waiting for me as well.

In the words of Alfred Tennyson, "'Tis better to have loved and lost. Than never to have loved at all." And, the moment to love and be loved again has been sweet.

There's beauty in recognizing even with a life partner,
I will still, in fact, die alone.

Hate to break it to you.

Do the work.

I used to look at relationships as a take-it-or-leave-it scenario. You take my unrealistic expectations of love, tendency to compare my relationships to everyone else around me (including people on social media), and my inability to pivot fights, or bust. The right one will completely accept me for who I am, flaws and all. My existence was good enough without a need to change, grow, or reassess how I steer relationships. I'll admit, I used to be pretty bad.

My view on boundaries, "What boundaries? You tell me everything, and we move about life as best friends without secrets." I maintained relationships like that for years, and then I learned of my own disposability. I know many don't like to hear this, but unlike the expectation that love has no limitations, someone will leave because of your unwillingness to compromise or understand their boundaries, regardless of how thick that booty is.

It took years of learning the parts of me that were toxic in relationships to have the maturity in my current relationship. I was unwilling to change until I realized that people in my life wouldn't necessarily like everything about me regardless of my intentions. Instead, the compassion and patience that came with working towards an understanding shifted my mindset to what love looked like beyond the superficial.

I always use my relationship with my parents as reference

since it's the longest relationship I've ever had. When you're a child, your parents are the smartest, most understanding, and patient people (for the most part). At a certain point, the roles reverse and now you're talking to them about your terrible childhood and new boundaries at Thanksgiving dinner. The evolution of this relationship shows me the continuous dynamic that no matter what type of relationship, love requires maintenance.

I didn't have to come whole, I just had to be willing to listen and respect what my partner was saying. We're all battling something: family issues, trauma, disappointments in other interpersonal relationships, road rage, excessive spending habits, drugs, sex, couponing, or having Hulu with commercials, and that's on top of loving multiple people.

Once you see the conditionality of love, it's easier to see what it mutually requires to be successful in it.

Well, shit.

"It'll happen when you least expect it."

Acceptance grants opportunity.

I was at a friend's family event, and as we sat by the fireplace, her sister said, "It'll happen for you one day," after another conversation about why I decided to be single. Once she said it, I had a moment of transparency. "Is this where I am in life? The 'it'll happen' stage?" There's something that's never comforting when people in relationships reassure you that singleness is temporary.

After I decided to no longer look for a relationship, I noticed people's reactions varied:
Some pitied me for being single.
Some assumed I was lonely.
Some suggested I was too dominant or difficult.
Some assumed there was something wrong with me.
Some judged me for my past and scorned me for my divorce.
And others gave unhelpful advice like, "It'll happen when you least expect it."

A running trend was that many opinions and suggestions came from people who'd never had to navigate dating in their 30s. The irony was a lot of those who gave advice had missionary sex in between commercials and left passive aggressive notes on the refrigerator. Some were on autopilot while others swept big conversations under the carpet to avoid another feelings talk.

It felt like they were only regurgitating what they saw on

Instagram or a woman's magazine instead of realizing they wouldn't and probably never do follow it themselves.

I hated the "It'll happen when you least expect it," aside from it contradicting "get back out there" and it meaning I had to do nothing but wait. So, I'm just putting money in the meter and BAM?! Or spread eagle at my waxing appointment and BOOM? It didn't seem likely, although I did match with an old massage therapist, but I couldn't get over the thought that he'd already touched my whole body before going on a date. Applying logic, it didn't make sense. It was only going to happen because I would make it happen, but then it didn't.

And then I met someone unexpectedly. Now, I'll give my relationship people the benefit of the doubt. I did meet someone when I wasn't expecting it, but I don't think it just happened on a whim. Instead, I think once I accepted whatever the universe was going to give me, whether it be a beautiful man or a cold, I granted myself the opportunity to shift my focus to everything else but a relationship, which, in turn, made me more available for it to happen.

I had no expectations of anything, which led to my "come what may" attitude. Oblivious to the idea that someone was interested since I wasn't looking for it, I didn't know when it was actually happening. I really thought those random DMs were just check-ins. My energy was a walking billboard for emotionally available men, and I'm out here enjoying trash television, walking my dog, and starting a new career in teaching comedy. Allowing everything welcomed everything, which made me lean in further.

Now, in a relationship, I'm the one giving the advice.

It wasn't that long ago I was getting the consolation arm rubs and faces of disappointment for a life of solitude, so I get it. I completely know the feeling of family and friends constantly discussing your relationship status and the frustrations of wanting it so badly. Instead of listening to people who have no idea what it's like to date or the perils of being single, remember:

"What's meant for you will always, always find you." -Tosha Silver
"Don't take criticism from people you would never go to for advice." -Morgan Freeman
"A busy, vibrant, goal-oriented woman is so much more attractive than a woman who waits around for a man to validate her existence." -Mandy Hale
"Bitch better have my money" -Rihanna
"Being single is definitely better than being with the wrong person" -Hassan Choughari
"I used to think the worst thing in life is to end up all alone. It's not. The worst thing in life is to end up with people who make you feel all alone."-Robin Williams

"Are you really lonely or
do you just need a little snacky snack?"
-Nikki Frias

Let there be no confusion.

He wanted to, and he did...

I've always made excuses for men's mediocrity. I'm certain it's muscle memory by now, but it was the worst when I was dating. "He must've been busy with work," after I didn't hear from him for a couple of days. "He's probably really tired," after planning a second date at his house. "Maybe he lost service," when I texted and got the green bubble of doom.

It wasn't until I experienced a man who was intentional (the kind that we both agreed on) with me that I understood the "if he wanted to, he would" narrative. For context, when I met my boyfriend, I thought he was asking me a lot of questions to potentially be on his podcast. We met through Instagram, and it wasn't random for someone to message me about comedy.

"Girl, I love you, but why would he want you to be on his podcast?" My best friend said after I confidently thought I was making a new friend. In her defense, his podcast had nothing to do with comedy, writing, or anything I can specifically speak on.

We had planned a coffee "date" for a week after we chatted. He'd had prior engagements and, having no expectations since being out of the game for months, I had no qualms. We chatted every day after that first introduction, and it moved to texting. Again, no qualms since it wasn't the first time I'd met someone who wanted to pick my brain on a joke idea or concept. As the days got closer to our meeting for coffee, one night while in the city he texted me randomly asking if I was open to grabbing a drink. "Hey, I know this is last minute and if you are uncomfortable with it, I understand, but would you like to grab a drink tonight?" It was at this moment, in the middle of my improv class, I thought this might be more than a podcast interview.

I could hear my best friend in the background, "I love you, but why would he want you on his podcast?" It made more sense since comedy was not his forte, though he did love it. I took a minute to pause on the "yes, and-ing" and replied, "Sure." His response was immediate, with a time and a location. We met at a very trendy bar full of corporate people getting wasted on a Tuesday night. It was very swanky, and the music playlist was a vibe. We sat down to talk and shared surface-level stories until the second drink. We closed down the bar, talking about upcoming goals and random talents over Erykah Badu's "On & On" and he walked me to my car. Once I got home, I thanked him for the evening and didn't think much of it after. He responded, "I'll see you Saturday." I obliged with no expectations of what that meant for us or my future.

We texted consistently after the first meeting, and during one of our conversations, we talked about our ideal day. As a writer, my day consisted of a coffee shop and writing my third consecutive New York Times Best Seller, and his showed sentiments of doing something he loved. Completely forgetting that conversation, a day later he randomly sends me a picture of a table and a computer someone stepped away from at a coffee shop with the message about "my perfect day" and a gift card for a cup of coffee and pastry. It was such an unexpected gesture and very kind. I thanked him.

A couple of days later, we met for our second unofficial date. This time, I was nervous. I was a little early and waited out front, unsuspecting of which side of the street he was coming from. As he walked up, dressed stylishly with a beanie and glasses, I noticed he was holding something. "I have a gift for you." It was a coffee mug from that shop, and that's when I knew he was going to get this coochie. I'm kidding. That's when I knew what someone intentionally being in your life looked like.

Since then, there have been multiple times I noticed this person considers me. Whether it be something I've said in passing that he's remembered or things he picks up that made him think of me. Dating someone who works toward making me happy was something that was so blatant I couldn't ignore. I say blatant because I used to try and find ways for the not-so-noticeable things that other men didn't intentionally do as "things" that meant they liked me more. I'd make an excuse or legitimize his behavior instead of just saying the truth: that they just weren't that into me, I was the afterthought, a person to pass the time, or just a needed distraction from something.

I once heard someone say, "If he likes you, you will know, and if you're confused, he doesn't like you." I couldn't justify the confusion once I experienced someone liking me and making their intentions clear. It was confusing only because I didn't want to accept the reality that the potential of this person stopped at Olive Garden or after 3pm every day of the week. No person who wants you

will risk losing you over some bullshit. Of course, there are limitations like work, kids, or time that can impact the amount of things people can do, but even then, there will be explanations, effort, and understanding without question.

Finally.

Allow me to reintroduce myself, again.

The discomfort that comes with change is natural.

For the past 20 years, give or take, my job has been entertaining friends through jokes and storytelling. As the funny friend of the group, my responsibilities included showing up late to events, being the life of the party, and spilling the juiciest tea about my dating life (like funny sexual encounters, embarrassing moments, and many stories of being lost in love).

I've always prided myself on being an open book. Aside from actually writing a book of all my business, it's not uncommon to find me talking to strangers about being a size queen or my mortgage rate. I'd dissect every intricate detail and have hour-long conversations about what it could potentially mean or hypothesize every action to anyone who'd listen. But the added pressure of reiterating the same story to multiple people began to take a toll on me with every conversation centered around who I was dating. I could see people live vicariously through my experiences, and it became the focal point where there was no room left for the other great things happening in my life.

I wanted to take off the funny friend mask. No more joking about that one guy or rehashing another first date fail. I set a precedent of giving unnecessary details and cliffhangers about dating. It was all anybody wanted to talk about, and it was exhausting. I understood this was my doing, but there are many other layers deeper than the funny girl persona. I live my life rather unapologetically, and comedy is definitely at the forefront of my personality, but there's reason behind it.

Being funny has its advantages, like invitations to events and free stuff, but more than anything, it also allows me to mask my own emotions. Comedy is a mask to hide the conversations I don't want to have and a safe space when I'm uncomfortable. Personally, making jokes and avoiding hard conversations with a punchline are easier than the alternative. I'm emotional, empathetic, and highly sensitive, and I've curated the relationships I want with my own personal limitations. Some people in my life only know one side of me on purpose. So, the quieter, less sharing, and private Nikki in a relationship might come as a surprise, but I've been evolving long before I had this man.

My life changed when I decided to move to New York City. One of the ballsiest things I've done. It forced me to a place of survival. I also changed when I lived alone for the first time ever at 28. It made me accept silence and learn the value of not always having the last word. I changed when I moved back home. It made me accept that sometimes you must go back to move forward. And to where we are now, taking a chance at finding love again reinforced what I deserved and empowered me to be more confident in my skin. My life has continuously changed with each new hard thing I've endured, and I've changed beautifully as a result.

For now, I'm keeping special things for myself and not taking the opportunity to have a TED Talk at every compliment, intimate moment, or spark of joy. I shared so much of my life after my divorce, and as I've continued to grow into my own, I understand not everything needs to be everyone's, and that includes my interpersonal relationships. The discomfort comes from people curious about my decision to love more privately. I'm no longer in a place to change or control other's expectations of me as the funny girl.

My best friend always says, "Change is not a bad thing," and for someone who has relied on being the same for so long, I'm proud of myself for accepting I am different through life's disappointments, beyond love, and how I've decided to better myself. Beyond a revenge body or a Pinterest board of affirmations, I am convinced of my power with or without a relationship. There's no guarantee we won't break up (kidding), but for now, it's fun loving autonomously.

Change is inevitable. What matters is how we decide to take the lessons and do the work to better ourselves. It's very easy to get caught up in storytelling when in a relationship, but know people will always be drawn to entertaining stories for their own reasons. New boundaries are new, and people can be uneasy about it.

Always make the best decisions for yourself.

35.

My one truest love.

You ever see the things online that say, "Remember that you once dreamed of being where you are now?" At 35, I never expected to be living out my purpose of bringing people together with comedy.

Throughout my life, comedy has always been there. I choreographed and performed songs as "Sporty Spice" at Minnieland, sang lead of "Leader of the Pack" by The Shangri-Las at the 8th grade musical, and, as of late, performed improv to a room full of strangers at a recent open mic night. I knew my gift was making people laugh, but for years I wondered how I could align my passion with a purpose.

I tried plays, improv troupes, open mics, and even TV acting for years in hopes that something would jump out and show me I was moving in the right direction, but nothing ever did. I traded my dreams of writing for SNL and taking comedy classes in NYC for a corporate life that provided a 401k and floating holidays. I made the hard decision that my humor was only meant to entertain my friends, family, and strangers in lines at the grocery store – until I started writing.

My first piece was an open letter posted on Facebook to anyone grieving. It got back a few responses from random nosey friends, but one in particular stayed with me. It was from a previous coworker from my job who said, "This is so beautiful Nikki, thank you so much for sharing your story." Unsuspecting that my words held any weight, she followed up with a message about how touched she was and how much she appreciated my vulnerability. After her comments, I kept writing as a form of therapy, and naturally, comedy started to trickle in.

I started a blog, wrote for some publications, and did the scariest: I wrote and published a book called *Does this Divorce Make Me Look Fat?* in 2022. Since then, I've met hundreds of women who've laughed, cried, and related deeply to my perspective on life and grief. I've never thought of myself as a writer. Instead, I'm someone who is reunited with her love of comedy through writing. For years, I've searched for a sign that I was living in my purpose, and it came to me without warning through the power of sharing.

This book emphasizes my quest for finding romantic love and the lessons I've learned, but as I start the 35th chapter of my story, rediscovering my love of comedy has been the most fulfilling. The man is just a bonus.

It's been the utmost privilege entertaining you.

Yelp: Another honest review.

"And that's number two, baby!"

I'd rate dating 2.0 out of 5.0 stars.

A graveyard of blocked numbers and deleted messages. Online dating was a great first step in getting out there and meeting new people, but over time it made me feel bad about myself. I felt like Goldie Locks trying to find something "just right," but the bears had chin straps, the mattresses were from college, and the porridge was half-priced margaritas at happy hour. It didn't seem like much between the times I stayed up for a response I never got, the number of dates I'd planned, or the hours wasted on retelling my story. But, the aftereffects of dating multiple people online left me more bitter and unhopeful I'd ever find what I wanted.

On a positive note, the leftovers reheat pretty well, and meeting new people is great practice for job interviews and elevator pitches. Also, let's add the confidence boost of realizing there's someone online right now starting a conversation with "Hey Sweetie" as their opener. Surprisingly, what happened after I gave up helped me reassess what I wanted and gave me the clarity that it might not be as accessible as I initially thought.

I'd rate being single 4.0 out of 5.0 stars.

Singlehood is something we all experience at some point in our lives, whether we want to or not, and my efforts to be chosen became my obsession. I didn't want to be in my 30s still bringing groceries in by myself or die alone, yet my efforts led to nothing. After the mental roller coaster of searching, I was left with the embarrassment of a failed marriage and now the residual fears of unworthiness. My failed attempt at keeping a man forced me to be alone intentionally.

In that time, I learned about accepting the disappointment of people, appreciating the companionship already in my life, romantic relationships not guaranteeing happiness, and the fear of being unlovable actually being universal. I've also had the honor of humbling myself. I, too, can block my blessings, and sometimes no resolution is the solution.

In the eight years of being by myself, I ran the cyclical process of grief: first with my divorce, second with my new life looking differently, and now the concept that the love I dream of might come in pieces throughout my life instead of as a whole. And yet again, that's okay.

In the words of Alex, "You are finite," Armstrong, "You are a lot in the best way possible," and Cassidy, "You are the prize!" Listen to your friends, they see your magic. And do me a favor…**believe them.**

Word Search: Dating.

Because why the fuck not?

```
S D F A K H D C U F F I N G A S K L D J A K L S J D L K A J S D L A
J S D L K A S J D K L A S J D L K A S J D L A J S D L F U C K B O Y
D L K A J S D L A B R E A D C R U M B E R A J S D L J A S L D J A S
L K D J A M C N A B I S H I O A J S C R A M N D F A N S K J D N A
K J S I T U A T I O N S H I P D R L A S N D L A N O I W U E O A I H
S D J K Z N C L K Z X N M C L E Z M X C A M N S L K P S M C N Z S
J N E W P H O N E W H O D I S J L K L A S J R I P P E D J E A N S L
K A J S L K D J A J L S K D J A L K S J D L A K S J D E L A J D K L
A S D L K A J S D K A O I E U R I O A J D G A L E N T I N E S D A Y
H B O Y B Y E S C M N A O S H J A O S J P O A K S D P O A K S D O
P A K U D P O A K S D G H O S T I N G L E D O A K S D P A J S D P
O J A M O M O A P S J D P A O S J D P A A A P A S J D P A J S D O P
A J B D P O J A S D O P A S O P D K O A A S J R O S T E R P A S E D
P O A S J D D S S P S J D I C K P I C A J S D L A J S L D T I N D E R
J A M K D S J K J K S D K U U P K F J L D N F K J A H S D H A J L J
B D P R E P R E S E N T A T I V E O A P O J A M O M O A P S J D P A
D O P A S I N G L E L I K E A D O L L A R B I L L O P D K O A D P A
```

CUFFING	BREADCRUMBER
GALENTINES DAY	FUCK BOY
SITUATIONSHIP	TINDER
BOY BYE	RIPPED JEANS
REPRESENTATIVE	DICK PIC
NEW PHONE, WHO DIS	ROSTER
SINGLE LIKE A DOLLAR BILL	"U" UP
GHOSTING	

Acknowledgments

This book is dedicated to Cassidy for always making Valentine's Day (and every day) special. Alex for thinking of me, always. To Mom and Dad, I love you. To Mrs. Christine for having my back. To Kay for always being there. To he who will remain anonymous, thank you for being a beautiful inspiration. To Ellen, aka Ma, for sending a Christmas gift, every year, Griffin for his forever side-eye and the rest of my tribe.

Thank you for always listening, I love you.

Nikki Frias is a writer and comedian on a mission to remind women how dope they are. This is her second book, following *Does this Divorce Make Me Look Fat?* She's the creator of Girltellme.com, a publishing platform dedicated to the empowerment of women writers through comedy. Her articles have been published in Pop Sugar, The Daily Beast, and Forbes. To follow her writings and other badass women toward writer world domination head over to Girltellme.com.

Instagram: @girltellme_dotcom

Website: Nikkifrias.com